DATE DUE

NOV 1 2004			

Demco, Inc. 38-293

with "expert"
, and countless
can really use—
where you're

ides are written
ent grads from
.S. You'll find no
re—just stuff to
cademic, social,

FISHING FOR
A MAJOR

You might know exactly what you want to do with your life. Or you might have no idea at all. In either case, reading what other students think about finding a major that makes you happy can help you consider things you've not thought of. Find out how other students approach choosing classes, getting the best out of the advising system, thinking about a career and finding a passion—and you might discover more than just a college major. *($6.95)*

SCORING A
GREAT INTERNSHIP

Finding and getting a killer internship during college has no downside—you'll learn a ton, spice up your resume, meet new people, and hopefully get a few steps closer to knowing what you'd like to do with your life after college. This guide is packed with tips on how to find the best internships, get yourself noticed and accepted, and learn the most once you're there. *($6.95)*

FINDING YOUR PASSION
BEYOND COLLEGE ACADEMICS

Part of what college is all about is helping us to figure out what we like to do and what we might like to do with our lives. To really do this, you have to go beyond classes and academics, and explore your passions by getting involved in extracurriculars. Think you might like to be a journalist but hate your English class? Become a reporter for your college or local town paper. A life as a psychologist sounds like fun? You won't learn much about it in your psych class, but you might if you staff a counseling hotline. Pick up this guide and use it to help you find your passion. *($6.95)*

TACKLING YOUR
HIGH SCHOOL TERM PAPER

You won't escape high school without writing at least a few term papers. Whether you're a naturally talented writer or would rather go to the dentist than write a paper, pick up this guide to learn the best way to tackle your term papers. Written by students who've written more than a few papers in high school, this guide will help you get organized, choose the best topic, formulate your main arguments, research effectively, and write a clear and error-free paper. *($6.95)*

To learn more about **Students Helping Students™** guides, read samples and student-written articles, share your own experiences with other students, suggest a topic or ask questions, visit us at **www.StudentsHelpingStudents.com**!

We're always looking for fresh minds and new ideas!

Students Helping Students™

LEAPING FROM PUBLIC HIGH TO A TOP U.

First Edition

NATAVI GUIDES

New York

Leaping from Public High to a Top U.
First Edition.

Published by **NATAVI GUIDES**. For information on bulk purchases or custom promotional guides, please contact the publisher via email at sales@nataviguides.com or by phone at 1.866.425.4218. You can learn more about our promotional guides program on our website, www.nataviguides.com.

Cover design by Monica Baziuk.

Printed in the U.S.A.

Copyright © 2003 by NATAVI GUIDES.

ALL RIGHTS RESERVED.

No part of this publication may be reproduced, stored in a retrieval system, or transmitted in any form, or by any means: electronic, mechanical, photocopying, or recording or otherwise, without prior written permission from the publisher.

ISBN 0-9719392-6-8 1211

Library of Congress Cataloging-in-Publication Data

Jackson, Katharine.
  Leaping from public high to a top U. / Katharine Jackson.-- 1st ed.
     p. cm. -- (Students helping students)
  ISBN 0-9719392-6-8 (pbk.)
  1. College student orientation--United States--Handbooks, manuals, etc. 2. College students--United States--Life skills guides. I. Natavi Guides (Firm) II. Title. III. Series.
  LB2343.32.J33 2003
  378'.198--dc21
                              2002155893

A NOTE FROM THE FOUNDERS OF
STUDENTS HELPING STUDENTS™:

Dear Reader,

Welcome to Students Helping Students™!

Before you dive head-first into reading this book, we wanted to take a moment to share with you where Students Helping Students™ came from and where we're headed.

It was only a few years ago that we graduated from college, having made enough mistakes to fill a *War and Peace*-sized novel, learned more and different things than we expected going in, and made some tough decisions—often without having enough advice to help us out. As we thought about our college experiences, we realized that some of the best and most practical advice we ever got came from our classmates and recent grads. It didn't take long for the light bulb to go on: We started a publishing company and launched the Students Helping Students™ series.

Our vision for Students Helping Students™ is simple: Allow high school and college students to learn from fellow students who can share brutally honest and practical advice based on their own experiences. We've designed our books to be brief and to the point—we've been there and know that students don't have a minute to waste. They are extremely practical, easy to read, and cheap, so they don't empty your wallet.

As with all firsts, we're bound to do some things wrong, and if you have reactions or ideas to share with us, we can't wait to hear them. Visit **www.StudentsHelpingStudents.com** to submit your comments online and find our contact information.

Thanks for giving us a shot. We hope that the student advice in this book will make your life better and easier.

Nataly and Avi
Founders of NATAVI GUIDES and Students Helping Students™

the primary author

A graduate of Kettering-Fairmont High School in Kettering, Ohio, **Katharine Jackson** is a member of Harvard College's Class of 2004. A psychology concentrator in Quincy House, Kate's activities include singing with the Kuumba Singers, dancing with Expressions Dance Company, ushering at Memorial Church, and writing and performing in the Women IN Color Project. She is also a member in organizations such as Women IN Color, the Undergraduate Relations Council, and The Seneca, Inc.

Kate will never forget the difficulties she encountered— academically, socially, and personally—making the transition from her public suburban high school in the middle of Ohio to the auspicious gates of Harvard College. She passes on her experiences and insight in the hopes of helping those undergoing the same transition.

the collaborator

Adam Watson graduated from Chapel Hill High School and left his native Chapel Hill, North Carolina, to join Columbia University's Class of 2004. He is majoring in English Literature with a minor in Creative Writing and pursues his interest in writing by working for student publications, writing and directing short films, and working as a research assistant for journalists and authors. His love for Columbia is only exceeded by his love for New York City!

He is currently spending his junior year studying abroad at Cambridge University.

the contributors

Students from Brown University, Columbia University, Cornell University, Dartmouth College, Emory University, Harvard University, New York University, Oberlin College, Tufts University, Wellesley College, Wesleyan University, Stanford University, the University of Pennsylvania, and Yale University contributed to this guide.

author's note

Congratulations on getting into a top university. Your adventure is just beginning. The next four years will be some of the most difficult, challenging, exhilarating, and rewarding years of your life. You will learn things that will blow your mind. You will change and grow in ways you never imagined. You will have experiences that will completely alter your perspective on people, the world, and life in general.

One of the most important pieces of advice I can give you (taken from a website relationship advice column years ago) is KFOIT: Keep Fear Out of It. A top-notch university, talented students, world-renowned faculty, rigorous academics—it can all be very intimidating, especially if you're coming from a public high school. But it's all part of the learning experience. If you spend your college years being afraid of failing or of encountering a situation that you don't know how to handle, you'll be robbing yourself of some of the most enriching and exciting experiences college has to offer.

We invite you to open your mind, quell your fears, quiet your insecurities, strengthen your heart, bolster your courage, take a deep breath, and dive in. You have nothing to lose and a lifetime of wonderful memories and experiences to gain.

- Katharine

collaborator's note

You go to college to learn one thing—a new appreciation of life. Even if you forget everything else in this book, I hope that you carry this attitude with you into all your classes, activities, and social gatherings at your university. Here, you'll learn the skills you need to pursue your dreams. You'll never look at a painting, read a book, or even watch late-night T.V. in the same way again. You'll probably discover a wealth of new interests and tap into previously undiscovered talents as you explore new clubs, activities, cities, and, above all, new people.

Can you imagine a better gift than a new, more intense enjoyment of life? When I realized this, I felt less intimidated and more fortunate. And tuition suddenly seemed much more reasonable!

- Adam

contents

what it is

The transition from public high to a top U. can be difficult, stressful, and frustrating. You'll have to learn to excel in an extremely rigorous and competitive academic environment, interact with students from a dizzying variety of backgrounds, and wade through endless new ideas and opportunities. The first few months at any college can feel like a never-ending hurricane for everyone, but if you're making the transition from a public high school to a top-notch university, the hurricane can often be more intense and stick around for a bit longer.

This transition can also be an intensely rewarding experience. You worked hard to get accepted, and now you can finally enjoy what you've worked for. Arriving at your top U. equipped with the real-world knowledge and experience you've gained from going to a public high school can put you at an advantage in terms of being open to new experiences and tolerant of differences.

Making the transition from public high to a selective university is a unique experience for each student. You might have gone to a top-notch public high school and thus find yourself extremely well prepared for the rigor of college academics, or you might come from an environment where you weren't as challenged. You may have gone to a diverse school in a major city, an experience that prepared you for the kind of diversity in culture and background of fellow students that most top universities go to great lengths to preserve. Or you may have attended a school with a somewhat homogenous student body located in a more rural area. Whatever your background, you'll face unique challenges and find your own ways to get through them.

what it's not

Making the transition from public high school to a top university is not the most difficult transition you'll ever have to make. It may certainly feel that way, but try to keep some perspective and recognize that you can get through it. If you made it past the tough admissions committees, you're more than ready to take on this experience.

Remember also that you're not the first or only person going through the fears and doubts during your first few months at college. No matter what kind of high school you attended, getting adjusted to the academics, the social scene, and an entirely new community at your college will be challenging at first. The difficulties you encounter may be unique, but everyone around you is encountering their own difficulties as well.

This transition isn't something that should intimidate you. You're intelligent and interesting and exceptional enough to be accepted, and you're smart enough to figure out how to succeed. Recognize that you'll be challenged and surprised, and trust yourself to deal with the new experiences.

getting ready

You worked really hard all through high school, toiled tirelessly over your college applications, rejoiced over your acceptance letter, finished out your senior year, and made everyone proud. And now it's only a few months or weeks before you get to start living out your dream of attending the college or university of your choice.

While it's a great idea to relax during the summer before your freshman year—or to work and save up for school— it's also a good idea to spend some time getting ready for your first semester. You don't need to take summer classes or stay up until all hours of the morning reading Shakespeare or memorizing chemistry tables, but you should browse the materials your school sends you, check out the course catalogue, and, if possible, do a bit of reading. You wouldn't leave your prized '54 Chevy sitting out in the driveway for three months without taking it for a spin around the block or at least checking the oil. Think of your mind the same way: You want to keep it fresh, working, and well-oiled in preparation for the Indy 500 of intellectual gymnastics that you'll face once you arrive on campus.

LEARN TO EXPLAIN YOUR CHOICE OF SCHOOL
▼
DON'T WORRY ABOUT FEELING ALONE
▼
PREPARE FOR ACADEMICS
▼
DON'T SHUT OUT YOUR PARENTS
▼
CONNECT WITH YOUR ROOMMATE

LEARN TO EXPLAIN YOUR CHOICE OF SCHOOL

If you haven't dealt with it yet, you'll deal with it soon. The inevitable question that you'll have to answer about a hundred times at graduation parties, end-of-year banquets, the gym, the supermarket, and your job. It's usually asked by some well-meaning but thoroughly perplexed friend of the family or parent of a friend:

"Why are you going to [insert name of your university]? What's wrong with [insert name of local college or university]?"

Some people cannot imagine why you would want to spend so much money to go so far away when there are perfectly good schools within an hour of where you've lived your entire life. We've found that the best response usually involves your sweetest smile and a charming tone with an answer such as: "I wanted to have an adventure and try something different." Sometimes the questioner honestly wants to know your reasons for choosing the school that you did, but some may feel defensive, particularly if they or their children chose the local university. Be sensitive to the fact that they may be very proud of their choice of school and may take offense at the idea that you turned it down in favor of your chosen college.

collaborator's corner
▼
I ignored the passive aggressive remarks that acquaintances made about my decision to go to Columbia— I choreographed my 'smile-and-nod' routine so carefully, it looked like a ballet move. But when some of the people I deeply cared for questioned my choice, I felt like I owed them a real explanation. I told them of my general passion

for learning and described a few of my favorite authors who taught Creative Writing at Columbia. I also reminded them of the unique opportunities New York City offered a would-be writer and filmmaker. When I specifically explained that Columbia was right for me but not necessarily others, most accepted my decision.

▲

After getting that acceptance letter, the first thing you usually want to do is shout from the rooftops! Many of your peers, however, may misinterpret your excitement as arrogance, particularly if they aren't able, for whatever reason, to go to a school like the one you're going to attend. The last thing you want to do is unintentionally hurt or alienate someone you care about. Be proud of yourself and your accomplishments, but be sensitive to the fact that others may have worked just as hard, if not harder, to get into the local state university. It's probably best to share your excitement and pride only with those who you're confident will share your enthusiasm.

DON'T WORRY ABOUT FEELING ALONE

The idea of many of your high school friends staying together and living it up at the local university while you're going to a strange, new place can be somewhat worrisome. You're going to encounter new challenges and obstacles and you might feel that you'll have to face those challenges alone, without your support network of friends.

Don't worry. Your university will have lots of students just like you, anxious about leaving their family and local community, and worried about surviving at a tough college.

You'll make new friends and find a support network that can help you feel at home. It won't happen right away, and you shouldn't feel like a weak character if you catch yourself wondering if you'd be better off going to school with your high school buddies—most of us have these thoughts during the first few weeks on campus.

You might feel like some of your friends can't relate to the anxiety that you have about going to a tough university. The best advice that we can share is to give it some time. You and your friends are all facing new settings and are probably nervous about going away to college, not knowing what might happen to cherished friendships. Above all, continue to make the effort to stay in touch, be supportive, and prepare yourself for the fact that dynamics may change with your friends.

"A lot of my friends thought that I was stuck up or conceited because I chose to go so far away and to such a prestigious place. A lot of my high school friends cannot relate to truly being independent, as many of them went home every weekend. I feel as if I can no longer relate to all of my friends like before."

Junior,
Harvard University

WE TALK WITH...

Stanley Fourteau
Senior, Columbia University

What should public high school students do over the summer to prepare for their first year at top U.?

Well, the first thing would be to read everything your school sends you. That's really important. Most of it seems unnecessary, but there are usually important things buried in there that you can't afford to miss. I read everything Columbia sent me twice to make sure I didn't miss anything, and I'm very glad I did.

The other thing I suggest is to read one book on any subject that really interests you. Just make sure you pick something that you'll enjoy enough to finish and really read carefully. The summer before I left for Columbia, I didn't know what I would major in but I always loved science, especially physics, so I picked up Stephen Hawking's *A Brief History of Time*. It was less than 200 pages and read more like a *National Geographic* article than a schoolbook. I could easily have knocked it out in a weekend, but I found it so interesting that I read it very slowly.

Why do you suggest this?

Oh, there're tons of reasons. Reading this book over the summer helped me focus my interests and pick classes, but it also prepared me for college in general. It was the longest summer of my life and I don't know how I would have kept my mind sharp otherwise. I got to school eager to learn and I didn't feel sluggish like a lot of my friends who hadn't cracked a book in four months. I also think I impressed my Astro professor when I introduced myself after the first class and asked him a question relating to the book. I know this sounds superficial, but it really pays off to be on good terms with your professors, especially in your first semester at school.

Would you recommend this strategy to non-science majors as well?

Absolutely! Pick any book that interests you—it doesn't have to be nonfiction. If you really sink your teeth into *Hamlet* or *Beloved*, I'm sure you'll get a lot more out of your first literature class and earn a much better grade. And once again, the most important thing is that it will keep you bright and excited over the summer. It's such a small thing, but it's so helpful.

And you really think this is all a public high grad needs to do over the summer?

It was all I needed to do. You don't want to come to school tired and stressed out. And you also should enjoy your last weeks with family and friends back home. Don't tell yourself to do a thousand things to prepare for school over the summer because for one thing, you'll probably get overwhelmed and won't do any of them, and if you actually do them all, you'll wear yourself out before you even get to school. These two things—reading the material and one book—are easy and effective.

PREPARE FOR ACADEMICS

Probably the most challenging part of going from public high to a top U. is academics. If you're lucky to go to a public high with great academics and amazing teachers, this part of your transition will be less difficult. Still, give it some thought—there are a few things you can do to prepare and make your first few months on campus go smoother.

> *"I think the one mistake I made was not perfecting my study skills in high school. Like most good students, I did well in classes without studying all that hard. When my teachers talked about study skills I wouldn't bother paying attention. In college, study skills can make or break your performance. I spent the first few weeks on campus changing the way I study to make it more effective and efficient."*
>
> **Freshman,**
> **Emory University**

The first thing you should do is get a good idea about what your next four years will be like academically. Understand how each semester is structured at your school—midterms, finals, breaks, etc.—what types of classes are offered—lectures, discussions, tutorials—and what core curriculum requirements you'll have to fulfill. The more you know before you come to campus, the easier your adjustment will be. To help you get organized, here's a brief list of questions to consider:

- How many classes or credits are you required to take each semester? Can you take more than the requirement? Do you need special permissions? Is it common for students to take more/less than the standard course load? Sometimes students may take more than the standard course load during the first few years so that they can take a lighter course load while writing their senior thesis.

- Is there a core curriculum, or set of required classes, and what does it include? Are you required to complete any part of the core curriculum during your freshman year? Can you substitute higher-level courses if you have AP credit?

- In general, what are the rules about getting credit for the AP courses that you took in high school? What do you have to do to get it?

- Are there any special programs or majors that you're interested in? Are there any specific rules about declaring these majors? When, in general, will you have to declare your major?

- What is the process for signing up for classes at the beginning of each semester? What are drop/add rules?

- How does the advising system work? Are you assigned an advisor or can you pick one?

By August, your university will have probably inundated your mailbox with letters and packages containing everything you ever wanted to know about your new school—and more. It's very easy to throw everything in a pile and think: "Oh, I'll look at it later." If nothing else, check the information pertaining to your academics. It may seem uninteresting or overly complicated, but you don't want to miss anything important.

▼

In the month before my freshman year, I must've gotten three or four packages a week from Harvard. I opened one package with a small book entitled <u>Reflections on Diversity</u>. Annoyed that it wasn't my housing info, I threw it away. When I arrived, I discovered that one of the freshman week activities was a group discussion of the book with a faculty member, and my group was led by the dean of the college! After speed-reading my roommate's copy, I managed to get through without looking too stupid. Take-home message: PAY ATTENTION TO ALL PACKAGES.

▲

You should also take some time and scan the course catalogue before you come to campus. Look through the various departments and make notes on any classes that you think you might want to take. Some schools require you to pick your classes before school starts. Others have a "shopping period" when you go to all the classes that interest you before registering for the ones you want. Either way, don't wait until orientation to start thinking about classes.

If a certain class particularly interests you, try to contact the professor with any questions you have about the class. Faculty members are very busy and don't always have time to respond to their emails, but it's worth trying. Making contact with a professor has benefits—you'll get a rough idea of what that professor might be like, you might get a chance to do some preliminary reading and avoid being overwhelmed, and if the class is oversubscribed, you might have an edge on getting in. Give a prof a call or send a brief email explaining your interest in the class. While it's important not to go overboard and come off as a brown-noser, many professors love enthusiastic, excited students. There is nothing worse than lecturing to a room full of apathetic, half-asleep undergraduates. Many professors will respond well to your enthusiasm because you're reminding them of why they love teaching.

If there's a certain class that interests you and it has been offered in previous semesters, it might have a website. See if you can find it on your school's site—it might have some useful information, such as required reading, class topics, and so on.

DON'T SHUT OUT YOUR PARENTS

If you're nervous about your first semester away at college, chances are that so are your parents. They're probably having a hard time dealing with the idea of you going to college and not living at home anymore. Sending you off to a somewhat intimidating university may add to their feelings of trepidation.

Everyone's relationship with their parents is different, but we suggest that you make an effort to involve them in the process. Show them the course catalogue, ask for their opinion about which classes you might want to take, talk to them about some of the extracurriculars in which you're planning on getting involved. Feeling like they're involved in this part of your life will save them and you a ton of stress and potential conflict.

collaborator's corner
▼
I came to college thinking independence meant breaking away from my parents when, in fact, it taught me a new appreciation for all they offered. As they step down from

their role as rule-enforcer, you'll probably see new sides of them and feel free to discuss new issues with them. They can also teach you important things about doing your own taxes, setting up bank accounts, and other all-important details!

▲

CONNECT WITH YOUR ROOMMATE

Whether you'll be living with one or more people, definitely try to connect up with them over the summer. You won't find out that much about your roomie over the phone, but it will take some stress away from anticipation and will make the first few days of your interaction a bit easier. Unless you live close by, the phone is usually your best bet.

It's tough to find things to talk about with someone totally unfamiliar, and one good way to get the conversation going is to figure out who should bring what: Do you want to have a small fridge in your room? Does your roommate have a good stereo? What about a rug? Sharing common items like this will save you money, but be careful not to agree to things just because you want to get along with your roommate. If he or she wants to pitch in for an expensive item, like a stereo or a T.V., and you can't afford it, be upfront about it and offer a less expensive solution.

Try not to read too much into the first conversation. Everyone is on guard and cautious when they first talk, and neither of you is likely to be "yourself." Holding off on making judgments will help you adjust to your living situation easier—flexibility is a great thing to have in general during your first few weeks on campus.

getting adjusted

You and your family will never forget those first few moments on the campus. As everyone tries to get their stuff moved into their freshman dorm, it's hard not to just stand there with your jaw on the floor, taking in your surroundings. The people, the buildings, the grounds, and the scenic landscape of numerous minivans and U-hauls crammed full of boxes and furniture lined up in front of the freshman dormitories will probably remain in your memory forever.

The first days and weeks on campus can be truly overwhelming, particularly if it's your first time living in a campus setting. In this chapter we'll share some advice on how to deal with the initial adjustments, keeping in mind the particular issues that may hit home specifically if you're coming from a public high school.

GO TO ORIENTATION EVENTS
▼
GIVE YOUR ROOMMATE A CHANCE
▼
EXPLORE YOUR DORM
▼
MAKE YOURSELF AT HOME
▼
EMBRACE DIVERSITY

COLD

by
Diana Cohen
Senior, Tufts University

I crossed the Mason-Dixon line on my way to move into Tufts and breathed a sigh of relief that toppled trees in a five-mile radius. At last I'd escaped my narrow-minded high school, rigid parents, and hometown in Georgia that was eerily reminiscent of *Deliverance.* On Thanksgiving, my parents could visit *me* because I was never coming home.

But the first thing I missed were the words, "How are you today?" Then I started to notice the silence, how conversations ceased the second people stepped into an elevator and how everyone was so rushed they merely bucked their head or threw up a hand as they raced by without ever stopping to chat. I made dear friends on campus, but in general, Northeasterners seemed so cold and distant. I was accustomed to treating strangers as feeling human beings worthy of your attention and respect rather than robots that should give you what you want, when you want it, and to shut up in the meantime.

And other things were cold besides the people. I missed swimming in October, hot home-cooked meals, and the room I didn't have to share with a roommate who ran the AC full blast 365 days a year. When I tried to confess my homesickness, my new friends couldn't help but snicker at my southern drawl and inevitably commented on how it would only get colder until March. They couldn't understand that the weather wasn't the real issue because they never fully left home. Most students at Tufts grew up in the Northeast and could catch a train to Jersey whenever they needed mom to do their laundry.

I suffered through a pretty bleak winter and felt like I was a failure for missing home. Only a redneck could miss Macon, Georgia, I thought. I had a good year all in all, but I still raced home after my last exam that spring. I had to spend a month or two back home to recognize all the things I love about the South *and* all the things I missed about Tufts. I missed my friends and all the thoughtful students with diverse backgrounds from whom I had learned all year. I also missed the intellectual climate and often found Macon more boring than ever. And yet I felt at home.

Homesickness is okay. In fact, my time away revealed the two aspects of my personality, and I arrived at a deeper understanding of myself, my values, and my country. Since I couldn't have mom to do my wash and dad to handle my taxes, I became more independent and resourceful. My relationship with my parents took a 180-degree turn for the better. I now appreciate difference and therefore think about people, society, and a restaurant menu in a whole new way.

GO TO ORIENTATION EVENTS

"You might feel left out at first, probably scared and nervous, but hang in there. It may take you a few weeks, even a few months, but you'll find your niche. Your place to fit in is out there somewhere and you'll find it sooner or later."

**Junior,
Cornell University**

Whether it's spending a week in the wilderness, soaking in a broken tent with ten of your new classmates; building a house for a local community; doing the infamous "lap sit"; or just going to an information session, do as much as you can handle during the orientation period. We've found that it's best to just dive into your new surroundings and get exposed to as many different experiences, students, and faculty as possible. Don't drive yourself crazy trying to attend every single event, but don't stay holed up in your room pining away for those familiar faces from home. Remember that everyone, no matter how at-ease they may seem, is facing a whole class full of new peers.

GIVE YOUR ROMMATE A CHANCE

Whether your roommate is from a public school, a private school, or from a completely different type of school and from a different part of the world, the initial rules of engagement remain pretty much the same:

- Be friendly. Whether you're usually outgoing or keep to yourself, make an effort initially to talk to your roommate, to relate, and to just hang out together. You don't have to try to be friends, but making an effort to be nice will pay off.

- Give each other space. This is tough if you're literally sharing one room rather than a small apartment where each of you can have some privacy. If your roommate comes back from a shower, maybe you can step out for a few minutes so that he or she can change. Or if you need to make a private phone call, ask if your roommate won't mind giving you a few minutes. These are small gestures, but the effort counts, and your roommate might follow suit.

- Don't try to do everything together. If you click with your roommate, then by all means, hang out, go to orientation, and sit together in the dining hall. But don't force it—you'll have a long time to get used to and to get to know each other. Too much time together initially can potentially backfire.

In general, recognize that you don't need to be best friends, or even friends, with your roommate. If you are, great, but if not, all you need is someone you can get along with.

FIRST IMPRESSIONS

by
Nathaniel Jacks
Senior, Columbia University

My parents FINALLY left. As I recovered from freshman move-in shellshock, I wandered around my room inspecting every corner. I had yet to meet my roommate, but he had already unpacked and the picture of his hot girlfriend along with his hip posters spoke for him: I am much cooler than you are, no offense. He returned and explained that he had been hanging out with friends down the hall. I was stunned. Friends, already!

I felt like even more of a loser when I stepped out in the hall. In the middle of the hall, a guy strummed on a guitar, serenading the girls who sat in a semi-circle in front of him. I peeked into my neighbors' rooms to introduce myself and I noticed from their bookshelves that they'd already read half the books on the Intro to English Lit syllabus. I spent freshman orientation trailing packs of other students, silenced by the stories of their prep schools, world travels, prestigious internships, and their opinions on philosophers whose names I couldn't even pronounce. I hardly felt smarter when classes started. I sounded like a buffoon the one time I spoke in class and I spent ten times as much time on my work as these kids said they did. I could only think of one person as stupid as myself on campus—the admissions officer who let me in!

Two years later, I have stories of my own. I made Dean's List every semester and made a group of friends I hope to keep for life. For one thing, I'm not stupid and neither are the admissions officers. I also learned that the first weeks of college in no way define the rest of your four years. If you fall in love with the girl you sit next to in the cafeteria, congratulations; however, odds are you'll barely ever speak to her and your other orientation buddies a month later.

While many people come to college hoping to mold themselves into a new image, eventually we all let down our guard and our genuine personalities resurface. Once we stop trying to forge a "cooler" personality, we begin to learn from each other and our new environment and then we really begin to change. In a few months, you'll realize how much you've grown. You'll notice that you speak more articulately in class and you'll spot impressive books on your own bookshelf. And most importantly, you'll better distinguish between awkward posturing and real sophistication.

EXPLORE YOUR DORM

Some of your classmates who attended boarding schools will be much more accustomed to dorm living. If you haven't had much dorm experience, get ready to become intimately familiar with the joys of living in a college dorm.

Take advantage of the social vibe dorm life has to offer. If you need a quiet place to study, the library is usually your best bet. Leave your dorm room for relaxing and socializing. Investigate common areas in the dorm and find out what amenities your dorm might have to offer in the way of kitchens, game rooms, fitness centers, and practice rooms. These are wonderful resources to have at your disposal, as well as great places to meet like-minded dorm mates.

You should feel comfortable coming back to your dorm after a grueling day, and one way to ensure this happens is to get to know the other students living there. Make an effort to meet them, spend some time hanging out in the hall or the common area so that your chances of running into someone are greater. By all means, chill out in your room from time to time, but perhaps leave the door open so that others can stop by.

> *"I'd never lived in a dorm before and it was pretty overwhelming to have people barge in and out of our room during orientation. But after the initial shock, the dorm proved to be a great social setting. Don't worry too much about privacy, especially during the first few months of intense friend-making."*

Recent Grad,
Wesleyan University

MAKE YOURSELF AT HOME

Your university campus has an overwhelming amount of resources at your disposal. Spend some time getting to know what and where they are before the semester begins, so when it does, you'll feel comfortable walking around the campus. This is especially important if you're attending a large school—get to know where all of the major facilities are located and the best way to get there.

Explore the library, the gym, and the various buildings where classes are held. Check out food and atmosphere choices at the different dining halls. After surviving four years of lunches in your public high school cafeteria, you're probably an expert at figuring out which dishes are tolerable and from which you should stay away. Get ready to polish your skills even further—few colleges have gourmet food options, and if they do, you might run out of dollars or points if you eat them regularly.

Grab your roommate, the guy you met during your orientation, or the girl you ran into at the library, and do some exploring off campus. Whether you're going to school in a city or a small town, getting to know your community will make your college experience easier and less claustrophobic. There definitely will be times when you need to get away from your books, your roommate, or the campus food, and you should find places to go close by.

CULINARY DELIGHTS

by
David Feinstein
Junior, Oberlin College

When I came home for Winter Break, all of the adults had one question for me: "So how's the food there?" "The chef dries out the filet mignon a little, but you can usually trust the foie gras," I wanted to reply. What do they expect? The dining hall is probably the only place where you won't find any difference between your top university and any other college in this country.

The key is to get creative.

Know the salad bar like the back of your hand. Even if the vegetables don't look vine-ripened, here's a hint: If the produce looks old, assume the meat is, too, and it's a lot harder to get food poisoning from veggies. Tossing the salad can be problematic. I recommend taking two bowls, one filled with lettuce and the other with dressing, putting one on top of the other so that they form a sphere, and shaking them to toss the ingredients. Let them stare and drool while you enjoy your perfectly tossed salad.

For the second course, pick the most edible entrée and doctor it up at the salad bar and/or the spice rack. Nine meals out of ten will probably feature spaghetti and tomato sauce (i.e. catsup and ground mystery meat). Try asking for the plain pasta, grabbing a chicken breast from the sandwich/grill section along with cheese and vegetables from the salad bar to finish your pasta primavera. Too fancy? Take a bagel or an English muffin, spread tomato sauce over the top and add cheese. Throw it in the microwave for a couple minutes and you'll have better pizza than the dining staff will make all year.

There's no accounting for taste, and you may not appreciate my culinary genius, but be sure to experiment for yourself because you'll waste a lot of money and gain lot of weight ordering Chinese every night.

EMBRACE DIVERSITY

"College opened my eyes to people of cultural backgrounds not native to my rural hometown. It's been a great part of my college experience. Through these interactions I have been able to discover similarities where I thought there were only differences, and I am now able to relate to a greater variety of people."

**Junior,
Harvard University**

Your university will be filled with students from a variety of cultures, races, and nationalities, and social and economic backgrounds. Whether you're from a small midwestern town, an ethnic neighborhood in the Bronx, or a miniature United Nations in the heart of L.A., expect to meet a lot of people who are different than you. They may have thoughts and ideas that seem radical and might seem even a bit offensive. Be careful not to immediately categorize people by stereotypes based on race, ethnicity, socioeconomic class, or country of origin. We can promise you that you'll meet lots of people who challenge, defy, and drastically change your conception of their particular minority group.

If you feel that you're in the minority at your school, try not to be overly sensitive to how other people behave towards you. Without meaning to, the most innocuous look or comment can be perceived as very offensive or snotty. Let your guard down and open yourself up to different people. Those people with whom you never would have been friends in high school may become some of your best friends at college. You never know what you and they might have as common ground.

collaborator's corner

▼

I'm a fairly mellow guy and I tend not to worry about outward appearances. I sport the finest shoes twenty-five dollars can buy and learned how to tie a tie on my twenty-first birthday. Still, I worried about first impressions weeks before I left for college. What would I wear the first day? Who would I go out with on the first night? What should I first say to a professor I really admire? And so on.

Everyone thinks about 'firsts' but some obsess over them needlessly. You'll quickly forget the first people you went to the dining hall with on your ninetieth trip there a month later. By then, you'll probably be sitting with new friends and complaining about the food! Likewise, no one will label you by the group of people you go out with on the first night. Don't flatter yourself—no one remembers those kinds of details!

▲

Don't be afraid. Ask questions (politely). Be prepared to get answers that may be different from what you expected. Prepare yourself for the kinds of questions that well-meaning but ignorant peers might ask you and cultivate proper responses. Educate yourself. The ethnic organizations at your university probably sponsor all sorts of dances, arts performances, and dinners that will give you a chance to be exposed to other cultures and ways of thinking—go to them. Some departments may also offer classes and seminars about other races and cultures. Take a class in the East Asian Studies department, buy a ticket to a gospel concert, go to a Hispanic cultural festival, or attend a Native American art exhibit. You may never again be in such a wonderfully diverse setting. While it may seem strange and unfamiliar, this is the time to seize the opportunity to explore completely new perspectives and ways to see things.

"As a first-year at Wellesley, I felt very uninformed and provincial. I'd never left the east coast and there were women at Wellesley from all over the country and the world. At first, it was difficult for me to find people to whom I related."

**Senior,
Wellesley College**

WE TALK WITH...

Katie McGinigle
Senior, Tufts University

How was your social life as a freshman?

I'm a senior now and I actually made all of my close friends freshman year—it's amazing how many bonds you can form in such a short period of time and how tight they become. I think it has to do with the fact that everyone is encountering so many new things and learning so much at the same time that you grow up as a group. You really grow up together freshman year.

How did living near a big city like Boston affect your social life?

You'd think everyone would go off into the city and do their own separate thing, but ironically, I think it really brings people together. Tufts has a very close-knit campus. My high school, like most, if not all, high schools, was broken up by cliques. Things could not be more different at Tufts, and I think the city has a lot to do with that. As you explore a city, you meet so many new people and you become a lot less assuming when you see someone you already know at a place you never expected would interest them.

So you find Tufts much more diverse than your public high school?

Yes and no. I think the students are more open-minded and accepting. I may meet more students of diverse races at Tufts than I did in high school, but they all come from fairly similar economic backgrounds.

Any advice to students making the transition from a public high school to a tough university?

Smile a lot and never take anything at face value. Always try to find out more about people.

handling academics

If you graduated Valedictorian of your high school class, congratulations. So did many of your classmates.

Probably the toughest part of making the transition from public high school to a selective university is getting adjusted to an entirely new level of academics. However bright you are, you'll be challenged, you'll work your butt off, and you will, at one point or another, get lower grades than what you're used to. The key to succeeding in your new academic setting is trusting that you can do it and being extremely proactive about tackling the challenge.

CHOOSE YOUR CLASSES CAREFULLY
▼
FIND GREAT PROFS
▼
TAKE AN "I'D NEVER TAKE THIS" CLASS
▼
LEARN TO PRIORITIZE
▼
GET USED TO WORKING HARD TO BE AVERAGE
▼
LEARN TO READ FOR COLLEGE
▼
TACKLE PAPERS WITH A PLAN
▼
RECOGNIZE THE IMPORTANCE OF MIDTERMS AND FINALS
▼
DON'T CHOOSE A MAJOR TOO SOON
▼
USE HELPFUL RESOURCES

☞ PUBLIC VS. PRIVATE—WHAT'S THE DIFFERENCE?

So finally you're here, at your dream college, and so are hundreds of your new classmates. Some come from private or prep schools, many from public high schools, and others from religious, international, or other independent schools. So, what the heck is the difference—or, in other words, why did we bother writing this book?

Although every generalization has tons of exceptions, private high schools tend to do a better job of preparing their students for the rigors of top college academics. They usually have smaller classes, tougher requirements, and spend more time on writing skills. Sure, there are many, many great public schools that rival private schools, but based on our own experiences and those of other public high school students that were interviewed for this book, private high graduates seem to have an easier time during the initial adjustment to the rigorous environment of a top college.

Do these differences mean that if you went to a public high school you won't do as well as your private high school classmates? No way. The field is pretty level after the first few weeks and we've all learned that more than preparation, what really matters in college success are your effort and desire to make it all happen. And if you've made it this far, you definitely have both of those.

CHOOSE YOUR CLASSES CAREFULLY

You'll probably have a lot more flexibility in selecting your courses in college than you did in high school. Even those schools that require you to take a certain core curriculum will give you some degree of flexibility. Make sure that you know and understand what your requirements are and that you choose electives that are from different departments and disciplines. You don't want to be taking three psychology classes during your first semester, no matter how much you love psychology. Another good idea is to mix the formats of your classes—try to get into some lectures and some seminars, some larger classes and some smaller ones, where you'll have a chance to get to know your professors and classmates.

You may have to take placement tests to get into certain classes. And even if you were the top math student in your high school, you may have to start with the lowest level math course. Don't get offended—just recognize that the lowest level course is probably more difficult than the most advanced class you took in high school. Make sure to talk to professors, advisors, and upperclassmen about which classes are best for you in terms of difficulty and interest.

It's important not to be overzealous in your initial selection of classes. While you may have been able to handle a full roster of AP and honors classes in high school—in addition to all of your extracurriculars—the classes you will encounter at your university will most likely be much more difficult and require much more work. Try to balance your academic load in terms of interest and difficulty. While AP scores may exempt you from intro level classes, don't jump into upper-level courses unless you feel pretty comfortable. At the same time, there's nothing wrong with dropping upper-level courses a few weeks into the semester if you find them too challenging or decide you need a stronger basic understanding of the material before you take on the more difficult subject matter.

Since classes often fill up fast, try signing up for the maximum number that your school allows, then picking the best four or five, and dropping the rest. If your college has a "shopping period" where you get to sit in on classes before you register, take full advantage of it and check out as many classes that interest you as possible. If there's a class that you're absolutely dying to take, but it's listed as closed to freshmen or has very limited enrollment, try talking to the professor. You may not get in, but it's worth a shot. It's also a good idea to make the professor aware of your interest in order to better your chances for getting in next time around. Just make sure to have some good reasons for wanting to take the class.

FIND GREAT PROFS

"My professors are absolutely brilliant. They really motivate you to learn and the amount of information that they can pass on is incredible—it's like they hold thirty books on one subject in their head."

**Freshman,
Emory University**

Remember that amazing teacher who made your senior year statistics class the most exciting part of your year? Maybe not, but think of your favorite high school classes and, more likely than not, it was your teacher who made them that way. It's no different in college, particularly at a top-notch school that attracts some of the best faculty.

Search out great profs and try to take a class with them. If your professor is engaging, knowledgeable, and enthusiastic about teaching, you'll learn a ton, even if the subject matter itself isn't particularly interesting.

Word of mouth is a great way to learn about various professors and their teaching styles. Talk to some upperclassmen and see whom they recommend. Your resident advisor (RA) is another great resource.

collaborator's corner
▼
Sometimes you have to take a course to fulfill a requirement, but as a general rule, pick professors with good reputations rather than classes that conveniently fit your schedule. In my opinion, the professor matters much more than the subject matter of the course he or she teaches. Students at Columbia set up a website where students review professors—find out if your school offers something similar. In any case, try and glean as much information as possible from upperclassmen. If you're curious about a professor, try searching for his or her name in the library catalog. If his books sound interesting, so might his lectures. If the library has multiple copies of the work and many are checked out, I bet he or she has something worthwhile to say.
▲

In general, make an effort to get to know your professors. It can be extremely rewarding and inspiring, not to mention helpful, as you learn to navigate the academics at your school.

Befriending faculty members can also have important benefits for life outside of the classroom. You never know when you might need a faculty recommendation for an internship or grant. Professors are also a potential source of employment. Most of them are active scholars who regularly contribute to the literature of their field. It's quite common for a professor to sidle up to a few favorite students at the end of the semester and ask them if they would be interested in working as research assistants. Working as a research assistant for a well-known professor is great experience if you're interested in thesis work or an advanced degree, and it's a great asset to any resume.

Getting to know your professors requires effort. They will not be there to hold your hand and pat you on your back, and they will not come to you and ask if you want to chat. You have to make the first move. That doesn't mean that you should bang on every office door with a tray of freshly baked chocolate chip cookies and a pitcher of raspberry lemonade, but it does mean that you should go to some offices hours and chat with your professors after class.

Talk about the class material, your interests, and find out what the professor is researching outside of class. Ask for help and advice about how to approach the subject matter or a particular assignment. Even if your professor seems too busy—they all do—be persistent. Your professors are a key component in the quality of your college education and getting to know them will help you learn, be more engaged in the class, and understand what's expected of you.

ALARM CLOCK

by
Jonathan Feinstein
Junior, Wesleyan University

Beat this. I was teetering on the brink between a C+ and a B- in my freshman calculus class so I really went the extra mile studying for the final. I did everything right: I began studying two weeks in advance, approached my professor with my slightest questions, and even got eight hours of sleep the night before! It was an evening exam, so I awoke bright eyed and bushy tailed, studied all day, and showed up to the exam room twenty minutes early. The room was empty and I felt good about arriving before anyone else. But an hour later, the classroom was still empty. I checked the online exam schedule and sure enough, the exam had been at 7:30 am, not 7:30 pm as I had thought. Forget a B-, I thought, I'm failing!

I emailed my professor who, as chance would have it, had slept through an alarm and missed an exam when he was a freshman. He gave me an incomplete and rescheduled the exam for after winter break. Although I hated studying over the vacation, I passed the class and learned several important lessons about how to succeed in college.

Write everything down! A planner costs less than five bucks at any drug store and can prove invaluable. If you don't think you need one, you're probably disorganized to begin with and need one all the more!

Also, going to office hours pays off. Even if some seem gruff, professors usually want to help you as much as they can. I could never have passed Calculus without all the extra help during office hours, and I doubt my professor would have been as understanding about my missing the exam if he didn't already know me as a dedicated student.

TAKE AN "I'D NEVER TAKE THIS" CLASS

Your university most likely has an extremely diverse array of course offerings and, if you're up for it, this can be a great time to try something new. Not only will you able to choose from more advanced and specialized courses than in high school, but you'll also be able to explore entire departments in which you'd never set foot before.

Take some classes during your first few semesters that are completely outside of your usual sphere of interest and ones that you'd never thought you'd take. An art buff? Venture into the world of economics or consider taking a science class. History and politics are your fancy? Try a photography class or a writing workshop. Part of what makes your top U. so great is the huge number of interesting classes that are taught by pretty awesome faculty. If there were ever a time to explore different fields and challenge your usual preferences, this is it.

Don't miss this chance. Just because you weren't great at something in high school doesn't mean that you won't find it interesting at college. And if you take a class and don't do well in it, it won't kill you—freshman year grades don't have that much weight on your overall college transcript.

WE TALK WITH...

Olivia Perlmutt
Sophomore, Brown University

What was it like for you to leave public school and come to Brown?

When I first got here, I felt completely unworthy of the environment that I was put in not only because I was coming from a public school in North Carolina, but I was also accepted off of the wait list. This is a strange position to be in when you think about it. It seemed like everyone I was surrounded by went to a fancy private school or a small alternative place where discussions of abstract opinions were the norm.

First semester of freshman year, I shied away from any class with less than fifty people and felt quite inarticulate when trying to express my opinions during discussion sections. But as more time went by, I began talking to other people and realized they had the same fears and insecurities. Everyone thought, "I'm not intelligent enough for a school like Brown, why am I here?"

By second semester, I became a little less timid about the classes I took and participated a lot more in discussions when I knew I could actually contribute to them, at least in some sense. I finally realized that I could add to a discussion even though I didn't have all the vocabulary or background information that some had. And the more I spoke, the easier it got.

LEARN TO PRIORITIZE

There will be weeks when you're able to get everything done and turn in all of your assignments on time. But there will also be weeks when things pile up and not everything goes as planned. The only way to survive is to prioritize by determining what absolutely must get done and what can wait.

> *"This is a simple suggestion, but I found that having one of those big desk calendars was extremely helpful. I'd write down the major to do's—like papers, exams, etc.—and have a picture of the whole week or month all in one shot. It made it easier to see when an avalanche of work was coming and prioritize what I had to get done."*
>
> **Recent Grad,**
> **Wesleyan University**

If you've made it into your university, chances are you're an over-achiever and somewhat of a perfectionist. Leaving things undone or turning papers in late is not something you did often in high school. But there will be times when you may have to make a trade-off and finish a critical assignment at the expense of a less important assignment. Few of us got through our first year at college without having to do this, and there's nothing wrong with it. Academics at your university are tough, and there are times when you have too many papers, exams, and assignments due all at once. Think about it, make your best judgment of how long it will take to get each done, and decide if you need to put something off or do it less thoroughly to get the more important stuff done.

Remember that some of your professors might be willing to give you an extension, if you ask far enough in advance and they're feeling generous. Most professors will inform their students of their policies on extensions during the first week of class. You should NEVER put your hand up on the first day and ask the professor about the policy on extensions because it will brand you as a slacker right away. Some professors leave it up to the discretion of their teaching assistants. Take a shot and ask, but don't make it a habit.

> *"When you first arrive, you're scared that everyone else will be these geniuses. And there are a few of them, but the vast majority of other students are ordinary human beings. The difference is how hard they work. You decide how hard you choose to work on your academics and how much time you want to leave to do other things with your life. Everyone finds their place."*
>
> **Senior,**
> **Stanford University**

You'll get the hang of it after a while and figure out how to prioritize and get your work done. One thing that will help is finding a study style that works best for you and for different assignments. Some of us need complete silence to get work done; others do better studying in groups. Some people can sit down and write a paper all in one swoop and others need to take a break every so often. Try a few things and see what lets you get the most work done in the most efficient way.

CATCHING UP

by
Jamay Liu
Sophomore, Brown University

I think the toughest part about making the transition from high school to college is getting used to the idea that your work will never "be done." In high school, work was mostly short-term. If you finished your weekend's homework, you could go out and have fun, without unfinished work or a guilty conscience hanging over you.

In college, professors hand out syllabi on the first day of class that outline the semester's workload. Oftentimes, the grade you receive for a course depends only on a few exams and papers. Readings are assigned, but usually, there is no one to check up on you or quiz you to make sure you've done them in time—it is easy to get by without having done the reading for large lecture classes. It's also very easy to fall behind.

It is really up to you to keep up with the work. College is all about learning how to manage your time, to sit down and do the reading, knowing that it isn't "due" for a week, but that it is best to get started on three hundred pages now. College is about realizing that oftentimes, you can't "finish" work—that there is always more to be done. (Actually, you find that in college, a lot of people spend an entire semester "catching up.")

It often comes down to decisions—should I go out, even though it's Tuesday night, since I don't have to turn in anything for any of my classes tomorrow? Or should I stay in and tackle the reading assignment I have for my comparative literature class? Learning how to manage your time is definitely an important part of your transition to college and really what marks the difference between high school and college. In college, you're on your own.

GET USED TO WORKING HARD TO BE AVERAGE

"Not being the best student was hard for me at first. When I arrived, I was blown away by how talented my classmates were—in academics, sports, music, other things. The one thing that I could do well was work hard and get good grades. But everyone else could, too."

**Sophomore,
Brown University**

A dean at a top private university once said to the parents of incoming freshmen: "We've never been able to fix the fact that half of the class is in the bottom half!" If you made it into your school you were probably never even close to the bottom half of anything (except maybe the swimming pool) in your entire life. Well, you might have to get used to it because, chances are, you'll end up in the bottom half of one of your classes.

This isn't fun and it's not something that's easy to get used to. But try to recognize that scoring the mean or below the mean doesn't mean you're a bad student or that you're stupid. Don't beat yourself up for it. Remember that you're competing with some of the best students at one of the best universities. Some of your classmates who went to private or prep schools may be initially better prepared to deal with the academic challenges.

"The caliber of university students' initiative and performance is, in general, higher than those of high school students. You definitely find that

ambitious, hardworking students make up a considerable proportion of your class."

**Junior,
University of Pennsylvania**

In fact, one of the biggest advantages that private high school students have on their side is confidence. They're used to dealing with advanced classes and complex subjects, to talking before small classes filled with bright students. They know how to make up for any lack of understanding with confidence. You may have the best ideas in the world, but if you don't present them well, it will be hard for others to understand and appreciate them.

"Like any college student, you must be prepared to work a lot harder than you did in high school. Depending on what your high school was like, you may have to work even harder than the average student. But remember that there is a reason why you've been accepted to this school."

**Sophomore,
Dartmouth College**

Don't be intimidated by your classmates, but do pay attention to what they say and how they say it. You will learn soon enough how to take a tiny piece of knowledge and expand it into a full-scale argument. Pay attention to the people who seem to give well-crafted responses in discussion sections or in class. How do they present their arguments? What makes their arguments compelling? It can take a while to gain enough confidence to speak comfortably in class, but give yourself time, be observant of how other people present their thoughts, and take some chances.

> *"Private school grads were a lot more confident in philosophical discussions in my section freshman year. After all, they were more familiar with that format and had often been exposed to readings of Mill, Kant, and Aristotle in high school."*

> **Junior,**
> **Harvard University**

It might take some time for you to figure out how to excel in your new rigorous academic environment, but you will figure it out. Keep reminding yourself that if you're smart enough to get into your university, you're smart enough to do well.

Be patient. Don't be too proud to ask for help from your professors, advisors, or teaching assistants when you need it. And don't despair if you get a grade that you've never seen before—it will definitely get better.

> *"I was pretty shaken up when I received a "B" on my first essay. I think realizing that I was behind was very motivating for me. I went to my professor's office hours and got a writing tutor and found that I was able to catch up quickly once I knew what was expected of me."*

> **Senior,**
> **Wellesley College**

author's corner

▼

It wasn't until the first semester of my sophomore year that I finally scored the mean on a midterm. My midterm scores had steadily progressed from the beginning of freshman year onward, placing me at the mean at the beginning of sophomore year and taking me beyond by the end of it. No amount of studying could've put me as an incoming freshman where I stood after four semesters. It was a natural progression achieved only through time and experience.

▲

WE TALK WITH...

Owen Whitehurst
Freshman, Emory University

What was the toughest part about making the transition from your public high to Emory?

I would say that one of the hardest parts is the realization that you're not one of the smartest kids in the class anymore. The first few weeks of classes at Emory were a little bit of a shock because I was not used to being in a room with thirty kids who all had different opinions that were all extremely well thought out and reinforced. Many times, at a public high school, you get used to the fact that what you say in a class will most likely be correct, or at least go un-challenged.

This problem, however, is not really a bad thing. It's a great motivation to work harder and learn more, as long as you recognize it as such.

Is that what you did?

I studied hard, but more importantly, I paid attention to my classmates. Remember, there is not only an extremely intelligent person in front of the class teaching it, there are also many intelligent people sitting next to you. By paying attention to what your classmates say, how they study, what their opinions are, etc., you will find that you're learning quite a lot.

LEARN TO READ FOR COLLEGE

You'll probably have more reading assigned for one of your college courses than you had for an entire semester of classes in high school. There will definitely be times when you get huge reading assignments and think: "I can't possibly read all of this in one or two nights!" Depending on what classes you take, the reading may also be very dense and difficult. It can certainly be very disheartening to spend several hours reading a dozen pages.

> *"In contrast to high school where reading assignments took maybe half an hour at most, college assignments require large amounts of time and skimming skills. I often have to decide how much of the assignments to do, whereas in high school I was usually able to do every one."*
>
> **Junior,**
> **Yale University**

The key to getting through your reading is not to read like you usually do. What you have to master is the skill of reading for college. And that means that you have to have a plan of attack for each book or article, you have to prioritize certain sections over others, and you have to master the skimming technique. Here are some specific suggestions:

- **Pay attention in class.** Your professor will either explicitly say which sections of the reading are most critical or will emphasize certain parts of the material that you then should understand in detail. Many profs like to assign more reading than is humanly possible to complete, but paying close attention to what they focus on in class can help you prioritize.

- **Get an overall sense of the material.** It's hard to read page after page of dense material without having a general idea of where it's going. Before you dive into any reading material, look it over to get an idea of what topics it covers, how it's organized, and what sections relate most closely to what's being covered in class or to your paper assignment.

- **Read the introduction.** It's a roadmap to the source and it will give you a good idea of the points covered and the order in which they're covered.

- **Prioritize.** If you're working on a limited time schedule—and you're probably always working on a limited time schedule—find the most important sections of the material and read those first. There's nothing like showing up for the midterm and realizing that the two sections of the book that you never got to are the two sections that are core to the exam.

- **Take notes or highlight.** This is really key. Taking notes or highlighting the material in your books or handouts helps you remember it better. Don't try to write down every single point, but focus on the main thesis of each section and its important details.

- **Skim.** We don't know of many students who graduate from college without mastering the good old skill of skimming. There's no secret formula for how to skim, but you might want to read the introductory section or sentence, and then read the first few sentences of each paragraph. Skimming is a great way to get through the parts of your reading that are not central to what you're learning about.

You have to be careful, however, and pay close attention to what your professors emphasize in their paper assignments and exams. Some profs have quirks like asking questions about material that was in the footnotes of the reading. Try to get a sense of what these might be and read accordingly.

- **Mix it up.** Your mind will get tired if you try to read a hundred pages of dense philosophical writing all in one swoop. Give yourself a break, go outside for a few minutes, change the setting, and read somewhere else. Also, mix up what you're reading—do some for your econ class, some for history, some for psychology, etc.

> *"I went to a very small public school, and upon entering NYU, I felt like I was really far behind everyone else. People had read books that I'd never heard of and I began to feel like I had slipped through the cracks somehow. I was just expected to know the stuff, or to work that much harder to catch up. It was quite an adjustment."*
>
> **Senior,**
> **New York University**

TACKLE PAPERS WITH A PLAN

Whether or not you had to write a lot in high school, writing college papers will be a challenge at first. They demand a much more thorough grasp of the material and need a strong thesis, well-articulated supporting arguments, and an intelligent and clear writing style. Even if you're a talented writer, getting a grip on how to write for college will take some work. We're not going to try and give you detailed advice about writing papers in a few pages, but we do recommend that you check out the Students Helping Students™ guide titled **TACKLING YOUR FIRST COLLEGE PAPER**, filled with practical suggestions from students who've been through the experience.

Here are some general suggestions about how to approach your first few paper assignments.

One of the most important things about each college paper is that it has to argue something. Whether it's a philosophical theory, an economic concept, a historical period, a comparison between two sociological profiles— whatever the subject of the paper—you have to pick a points and make a case for it. That point is called the thesis and it serves as the core argument of your paper. The purpose of writing a paper is to argue either for or against a certain point by analyzing the relevant information, presenting evidence and any related supporting details, and acknowledging but disproving the counterarguments.

> *"After my second econ class our professor told us that we had a five-page paper due in two weeks on the reading that we'd done so far. I was baffled—he didn't give a specific topic or pose a question. The few papers I wrote in high school were always in response to a specific question. It was one of the worst papers I ever wrote in college, but after working through it with the class T.A. the concept of having a thesis became permanently ingrained in my mind."*

**Recent Grad,
Wesleyan University**

When coming up with a thesis, a good strategy is to ask questions about the topic of your paper. Here's a quick example:

Topic: Economic boom of the late 1990s.

Question: What was the main cause of the economic boom of the late 1990s?

Thesis: Technology, specifically the Internet, primarily caused the economic boom of the late 1990s.

Once you have a thesis, you need to come up with arguments that either support it or go against it. Read through your class materials and, if necessary, do some outside research. As you read, refer to your thesis constantly—it will help you stay focused and prevent losing valuable time reviewing information that's not useful for your paper. Take quick notes on any important details, and make sure to keep track of where each piece of information comes from.

There are many different ways that you can actually structure a paper, but one of the most popular and one that works well for many disciplines is Thesis—Analysis—Argument. State your thesis, analyze it, and then present arguments that support the thesis and your analysis of them. Discuss arguments that might disagree with your thesis and explain why your thesis is appropriate even with the existence of counterarguments. Finish off your paper with a summary of your main arguments and your thesis. This is a very general idea, however, and you should customize it as necessary for different types of papers.

Most college professors are picky about grammar and spelling errors, so make sure to take some time to proofread your paper before turning it in. Even if you have half an hour before the deadline, print out a draft and go through it carefully.

> *"My classmates were on top of their paper-writing game. They all had their individual prep-school handbooks on how to write a paper and personal MLA guides ingrained into their head. Many could edit and revise papers in mere minutes. I've gotten along well, but, honestly, I still have no idea how to footnote! I've tried to follow guidelines from the MLA and most roommates, friends, and teachers are willing to help me out. Also, the writing workshop has really saved me—it's a great resource, so use it!"*
>
> **Sophomore,
> Brown University**

One of the greatest resources your university offers to help you with writing papers is a writing workshop. It's usually staffed with undergraduate and graduate students who can help you with everything from figuring out your thesis to structuring your arguments to making sure that your paper is written well and is error-free. Take advantage of this great resource and make an appointment. Many top colleges also publish guides or brochures on writing techniques. Learning how to write well is essential to your success at college and once you graduate, as we've all learned.

RECOGNIZE THE IMPORTANCE OF MIDTERMS AND FINALS

In high school, our performance was usually measured over the course of the semester with quizzes, tests, and papers, all of which added up to your overall grade, but none of which had the capacity to make or break it. In some public high schools, finals were a laughable ritual to which only the tragic few not lucky enough to get an exemption were subject.

In college, midterms and exams will comprise the majority, if not all, of your grade for each class. While it's important not to get too stressed about it, we recommend that you start studying at least a week in advance for midterms and final exams. If this seems like a ridiculous idea, wait until after your first round of exams and see if you still disagree.

author's corner
▼

I practically failed my first college midterm. After studying for weeks in advance, I took the test and thought I did pretty well. When we got our midterms back, much to my disappointment, I found myself at the bottom of the class. I thought to myself, "This is an intro psych class. Everyone here is taking psych for the first time. How could I score so badly compared to all these other first-timers?" Turns out there were a lot of upperclassmen taking it as an elective who knew how to study and how to get help.

After lots of tears, I finally went to my TF (Harvard's version of a teaching assistant or T.A.). To my surprise, I found her to be much more supportive and helpful than I had expected. She gave me some great tips on how to study for that specific type of test. I spent a good portion of my Christmas break studying for the final and wound up getting a decent grade in the class. I learned a lot about what works best for me in terms of study habits for that kind of subject matter. I also learned that a bad midterm grade does not have to mean doom for your overall grade in the class.

▲

Always ask your professors whether an exam is cumulative or just covers material after the last exam, but never make the mistake of asking: "What's on the exam?" Some professors will take this as your caring solely about getting a good grade rather than getting a grasp of the subject matter.

Past midterms and finals are GOLDEN. Some colleges may have an official website where they post old exams for each class. This is an invaluable resource. Professors usually change the questions year to year, but getting an idea of what type of material the professor emphasized and what types of questions were included can help you prioritize what material you review. If by chance you get a professor that uses most of the same questions every year, you will have given yourself an enormous advantage by studying old exams.

collaborator's corner

▼

When I first came to college, I thought I was so tough. I boasted of never getting sick and considered myself the Bruce Lee of sleep deprivation. I was determined to work and play harder than any other student on campus. I spent so many hours in the library studying for my first finals that I brought a change of clothes and a toothbrush along. I endured this hellish experience by dreaming of winter break. When my last exam finally ended and I returned home for vacation, I immediately came down with the flu. So much for my break.

Instead of learning from this, I worked just as hard at the end of the spring term. This time my body gave an even clearer signal that I was working too hard—I got pneumonia days before my first exam. I was too feverish to see the lines on the bluebook page so I had to take incompletes in several classes. Worst of all, I was alone in my dorm room without Mom to carry bowls of chicken noodle soup and cold glasses of ginger ale to me in bed.

Don't work too hard! In the first place, it's counterproductive—my grades suffered from my Rambo-like study skills. More importantly, there is a lot of worth studying in college OUTSIDE of that dreary library. Be sure to study, but take your toothbrush on more interesting trips than to the stacks!

▲

DON'T CHOOSE A MAJOR TOO SOON

Maybe you came to college knowing exactly what you want to do with the rest of your education and the rest of your life. Or maybe you're completely open to exploring new disciplines and ideas. Either way, take your time in figuring out your major. Most universities will give you until second semester of your sophomore year to declare your major, and you should take that time.

Try to explore at least a few fields of study that you know little about. How do you know that you don't have a bright and exciting future as an anthropologist if you've never taken an anthropology class? You'll learn something new and meet new people—even if you never end up taking another class in that department. There's no better time than college to experiment.

If, after a semester as a chemistry major you find that long hours standing over test tubes of funny-smelling chemicals aren't your thing, and you're not exactly thrilled about spending the rest of your life in a dimly lit lab with flickering fluorescent lights, look into the options you have for changing your major. You may be able to find a similar but more interesting major that accepts all of your chemistry credits and gives you a future that is more amenable to your lifestyle and interests.

And don't be afraid to study what interests you, as opposed to what your parents or other people tell you that you should study. It's understandable that you and your family worked extremely hard for you to get into your top U. And perhaps everyone, including your second cousin twice removed, can't wait to go to your medical school graduation. But guess what, they're not the ones who will have to go through medical school and live their life as doctors—you will, and you should make sure that what you choose to study is what you enjoy, rather than what you think you should be studying. Your feelings of obligation are completely understandable, especially if your parents are spending every last penny to send you to college, but recognize that if you're miserable and uninterested in what you're studying, they won't be happy either.

USE HELPFUL RESOURCES

There are a tremendous amount of helpful resources available at your school and they're eagerly waiting for you to use them. Take advantage of them—they'll make your life easier, help you learn better, and yes, help your grades, too.

You'll probably be assigned an academic advisor once you get to campus. Go see that person. Advisors can be immensely helpful in many ways—with logistics like dropping and adding classes, declaring a major, or with more general issues like helping you map out your plan of study. Advisors are great because they're an independent and somewhat objective third party. They might be able to point out things you haven't though of and can be a great sounding board for ideas, like pursuing an independent major.

Try to get an advisor within the department of your intended major. They can give you the inside scoop on which classes you should absolutely take and which classes you should avoid at all costs. They can help you formulate ideas early on for possible thesis topics and potential thesis advisors. And as we mentioned before in the section about getting to know faculty, they could become a potential source of employment for a research assistantship.

If you don't like your advisor or don't seem to get along, see if there is a way you can switch. Having someone to whom you can talk is important and you should feel comfortable with that person.

Another great resource are Teaching Assistants, or T.A.s, as they're affectionately called. Most of your professors will have an upperclassman or a graduate student working with them. T.A.s do everything from grading papers and exams to holding study sessions and prep sessions for tests—they generally know the class material well and can shed some light on the professor's quirks and pet peeves. Get to know your T.A.s. Talk to them if you have a question and go to a few study sessions to see if they're helpful.

"T.A.s are a huge resource! They do much of the grading and often know exactly what professors look for in papers."

**Senior,
Columbia University**

We've mentioned the writing workshop already, but since it's such a helpful resource, we're going to harp on it some more. It can really be a lifesaver, especially if you need to improve your writing skills. Make it a habit, at least at the beginning, to visit the writing workshop once for each major paper.

"My writing abilities were not at the level my English professor expected, and he wasn't enthusiastic to help me either. The writing center proved to be extremely helpful. I firmly believe that the three hours I spent there helped raise my grade considerably."

**Freshman,
Emory University**

Finally, don't neglect your Resident Advisors. Sure, their main role isn't to help you with academics but they've faced all the same challenges and probably can share some good advice.

Asking for help might not be what you're used to doing, but to succeed in your new academic setting you need as much support as you can get. Trust us. Getting advice doesn't mean that you're stupid—quite the opposite. Plus, you're paying big bucks for all of these resources and it would be a shame to waste them.

making the most of extracurriculars

Your university offers a tremendous variety of extracurricular activities in which you could get involved. And we definitely recommend that you do get involved in a few—you'll meet people, get a break from classes and homework, and maybe even find a new passion. (Extracurriculars are also great resume builders, but it would be a shame to get involved just for that reason.)

Be careful, though. There are so many options and different ways that you could get involved that it's easy to become overwhelmed and see your hours of sleep diminish and your grades start sliding south. So choose carefully, try some things you haven't tried before, and remember that you need to have some time just to hang out with friends and chill, too.

TAKE YOUR TIME
▼
SIGN UP
▼
GO TO INTRO MEETINGS
▼
ASK AROUND
▼
PACE YOURSELF
▼
TAKE A BREAK FROM WHAT YOU'VE ALWAYS DONE
▼
BALANCE
▼
KNOW WHEN TO STOP

TAKE YOUR TIME

The first few weeks on campus can be overwhelming as you're bombarded with information on various groups, teams, clubs, and organizations. There's also probably an activities fair to which you should definitely go and where overzealous upperclassmen will try to convince you that you MUST join their club, choir, organization, or juggling troupe.

Take your time and figure out what you really want to try out. Most of the time, you won't need to sign up and start participating right away, and you should get to know all of your options before committing.

SIGN UP

It doesn't hurt to put yourself on the mailing list of the organizations and clubs that interest you. The more information you get, the more you'll know about each activity. It's a good idea to keep an eye out for what's going on around campus that might interest you, even if you don't end up getting involved.

"In high school I was a huge fish in a very small pond. I did everything and did it well. When I got to college, I found out that about 500 other students had done everything that I did in high school and more. I realized that I was suddenly a tiny guppy in a very large ocean of sharks. It was very intimidating to even consider joining clubs, so I just

didn't. Looking back, it's something I really regret. I wish I had just made that much more of an effort to distinguish myself in college."

**Senior,
New York University**

GO TO INTRO MEETINGS

Most clubs and organizations will have an introductory meeting where you can come and hear about that particular activity and meet some of the people involved.

Although it may seem very intimidating to go to a meeting full of unfamiliar faces, it's a golden opportunity. First, you'll be able to ask any questions you have about the organization and the time commitment of being involved. Second—and this is really valuable—you will get a feel for the leadership and the other members. Who's involved in the organization and what they're like can make or break your experience. You don't have to be best friends with everyone, but you should generally feel pretty comfortable.

A side advantage of going to these meetings is the chance to meet other students with similar interests. Regardless of whether or not you ultimately become involved in the organization, you will have met many kindred spirits who may become friends over the course of college.

"I found new friends not through parties, but through the extracurriculars I participate in. That's what's so wonderful about a school like this—almost

everyone has something interesting to offer. And I realize that I, too, fit into this scheme."

**Sophomore,
Brown University**

ASK AROUND

Find out what people are saying about groups and activities that interest you. Check out what kind of a reputation the organization has on campus in terms of quality, satisfaction of those involved, and environment within it. While this last detail may sound odd, it's important. Whether you're someone who thrives in a competitive, fast-paced atmosphere or someone who needs a nurturing feel with a strong sense of community, you'll want to make sure that your activities can give you the type of environment that you need.

A great way to get the scoop on an organization is through word of mouth. Feel free to ask a few upperclassmen and see if you can find any past members—ask them why they aren't members any more. Just keep in mind that everyone's opinion is simply an opinion and is not necessarily representative of what your experience will be. If you can, try to get a variety of opinions to enhance your perspective.

PACE YOURSELF

This is probably the most important part of making the most of extracurriculars. While you may have been able to handle heavy involvement in lots of activities in high school, you will most likely not be able to function at the same level in college. The tough academics will take more of your time and the activities themselves tend to be more intense. You may ultimately be able to work your way up to handling lots of activities, but it's important to start small to give yourself time to get used to your new environment.

Recognize that the adjustment from high school to college may take more time than you think, and it's important not to schedule away every spare minute of your days. We recommend that you start with one or two activities that pique your interest. Most activities recruit new members at the beginning of the semester, so you can always change or add more activities halfway through the year.

"In high school, I essentially had time to participate in any extracurricular activity that I desired—I was active in several organizations. In college, however, my free time felt more limited, and I had to make difficult choices. I had to decide which activities were the most important to me and not do others."

**Sophomore,
Harvard University**

author's corner
▼
My activities have completely changed every semester. While I've enjoyed them, there are also many more that I

want to be a part of before I graduate. Constantly changing my activities has given me the opportunity to sample from many dishes in the college buffet and has given me a broad, rich college experience.

▲

TAKE A BREAK FROM WHAT YOU'VE ALWAYS DONE

Your university will have many opportunities for you to get involved with activities you'd never even dreamed about. Use this opportunity to try something you haven't yet had a chance to experience. Don't stick with something simply because you're good at it, because you've spent your entire life doing it, or because everyone back home defines you by it. College is a time to reinvent yourself if you so choose. There's nothing wrong with sticking with what makes you comfortable and happy, but don't let it hold you back if you're aching to try something new.

Try taking a semester away from your usual activities with the knowledge that you can always come back to them. You may get to college and find that you've burned out on playing oboe in the orchestra or your passion for riding the unicycle just doesn't interest you anymore and you'd much rather get involved with set design. Great! Try writing for the school paper to test out your lingering interest in journalism, or run for student office if you have thoughts of going into politics.

Extracurricular activities at some selective colleges can get pretty competitive, but don't let that stop you from trying new things. Don't be intimidated if some of your classmates seem more experienced or skilled. What you don't have in experience you can definitely make up for in effort.

author's corner
▼

My main activity in high school was performing. When an injury sidelined me from the dance studio for an entire year, I was devastated. I'd spent my entire life dancing and now the idea of facing a semester with no dance was absolutely horrifying. I joined the gospel choir in an effort to fill the void in my schedule and found it to be the most rewarding decision I'd made at school. After overcoming the injury, I'm back in the dance studio, but now I have a whole new set of interests and friends that I never would have gained without that injury.

▲

Do what makes you comfortable. While it's important to try new things and open yourself up to new experiences, it's also important to do what truly interests you and not surround yourself with people who stress you out. Be brave and take some risks, but pay attention to your instincts.

BALANCE

Striking the balance between being involved and being over-committed is a skill, and one that you should definitely learn. Unless you're blessed with an iron constitution that can handle no sleep, you'll burn out and get sick if you spend all of your free time running from one activity to the next.

The academic/extracurricular/social balance is also very important. What consumes most of your time will vary depending on factors such as an impending midterm or hellish tech week schedule for a theater performance. In general, we suggest roughly a 40/30/30 split in terms of time spent on academics, extracurriculars, and your social/personal life. Obviously there's no precise formula for how to organize your time, but just recognize that college is about more than just one thing or activity.

If you feel overwhelmed with numerous rigorous extracurriculars, you're probably doing too much. Don't feel like a loser who can't handle it and instead remember that you're in a new atmosphere with tougher requirements. Everyone needs some breathing room.

> *"The first year can be tough just because it's a lifestyle change. You're living in a different place, in a different way, with different people. It can be difficult to maintain the gung-ho attitude that most of us had in high school when the base parts of your life have been switched around. Who wants to worry about auditioning for a student group or taking on extra credit when you still haven't gotten the hang of the laundromat?"*
>
> **Senior,
> Stanford University**

CHOCOLATES

by
Rachel Kitson
Sophomore, Brown University

College is like a box of chocolates: You want to sample one of everything, but try too many and you'll get sick! I could scarcely say no to an extracurricular activity when I first came to school. "Actually, I'd love to join; I've always wanted to learn how to rock climb. Student Aeronautics Association, what's that? Sure I'll join it if I really get to fly a plane every weekend. The blowfish cooking club? Sounds great!" I made Rushmore's Max Fisher look like a recluse.

I'd stagger into a club meeting exhausted from class, homework, and work-study and expect to have the time of my life. Instead, I found cold pizza, name games, and an offer to attend the more serious organizational meeting next week. I didn't realize that to enjoy an extracurricular, you have to invest the time to learn the ropes and earn the seniority necessary to actively participate in it. The more novel the activity, the more time it requires.

Savor your college chocolates by focusing on one extracurricular first semester. Maybe try two, but if you won't have the time to develop any one interest if you try too many. Needless to say, your grades and social life may also suffer. I know how hard it can be to balance enthusiasm with pragmatics, but don't waste your precious first weeks of college running from quilting club to lightweight sumo wrestling tryouts like I did!

KNOW WHEN TO STOP

It's flattering to be actively recruited by campus organizations. But if you find after a few meetings that the activity isn't meeting your needs or that you just aren't excited about it, don't feel guilty about bowing out. Your time is too valuable to spend involved in activities that you don't enjoy and you won't be a good contributor if you're bored.

Make sure, however, that you can make a graceful exit without offending people or damaging an ongoing effort.

> *"In high school, I did every extracurricular I could get my hands on, and I still seemed to have enough time to get my work done. As soon as I got to Yale, I got my name on as many extracurricular email lists as I could. I wound up involved with a lot of activities, but it was way too much for me to devote the amount of time I would have liked to my classes. I also found myself feeling obligated to stay with the extracurriculars I started as a freshman, leaving me feeling trapped in a situation with too much to do and not enough time to do it."*
>
> **Junior,**
> **Yale University**

socializing

Maybe your high school social life consisted of Saturday nights with your eyes glued to the computer screen, churning out papers and college applications in hopes of someday gaining admittance to your top U. Or maybe your social life was more reminiscent of *Clueless* and *Can't Hardly Wait*. Regardless, the college social scene is a big change from high school.

Your social life in college is largely a function of the way that you choose to define it. We can give you a few tips and words of advice from our own experiences, but ultimately, you'll have to figure out what makes you most comfortable.

RECOGNIZE THE IMPORTANCE OF A SOCIAL LIFE
▼
GET OUT THERE
▼
DON'T BE INTIMIDATED
▼
MAKE YOUR OWN CHOICES
▼
GET OFF CAMPUS
▼
WATCH YOUR EXPENSES

RECOGNIZE THE IMPORTANCE OF A SOCIAL LIFE

Adjusting to college is hard, regardless of what type of high school you attended. You're going to miss the friends you grew up with. Even if you weren't that social in high school, you still lived at home, surrounded by your family, and someone was there to keep an eye on you. You may have also had friends or neighbors who watched you grow up and were always around.

At college, you're without your old network of parents, friends, and acquaintances. Unless you're extraordinarily independent, the only way to survive is to develop a college "family" in the form of your friends. It's important to put some effort into making friends and creating a supportive circle of peers and advisors.

As we've said before: Do what makes you comfortable. Get out there, meet new people, make new friends, but know when to give yourself a break and take time for yourself. You don't need to know the entire campus—a close-knit group of a few friends is what you may cherish most.

"Balancing your social life and your academics means sometimes putting your social life first."

**Senior,
Harvard University**

GET OUT THERE

"It's easy (and somewhat unavoidable) to make friends with the people who live close by, but it's even more important to get out and meet people with whom you have common interests, not just similar addresses."

**Senior,
Harvard University**

It's easy to feel overwhelmed during the first few weeks on campus. Everyone seems so friendly and outgoing, and you're meeting new people every few hours. Some of your classmates may be from families that moved to a different part of the world every few years and are more used to being in new, unfamiliar situations where they have to make friends quickly. Some of them might also come from one of those schools that sends twenty students to your college every year and may come with an already-made group of friends.

The best thing to do is just get out there and meet people. Go to as many events as you have the energy for and try to attend different kinds of events so that you bump into a variety of people. If there's nothing going on or you just don't feel like going to yet another ice-cream social sponsored by some obscure organization, go for a walk around the dorms and see who you run into. There's nothing wrong with being friendly. Not everyone will be receptive, but you'll find many people who are eager to get to know you.

"Don't shy away from making friends with people of different backgrounds and personal interests. While a public school may possibly have more socioeconomic and ethnic diversity than a private school, it's amazing how quickly students seek out others like themselves and fail to branch out. Going to a large university presents diversity on an even larger scale, so be sure to embrace it rather than shy away from it. Being a football-playing fraternity brother doesn't mean you can't or shouldn't be friends with an a capella singing member of the Fine Arts Club, nor does it mean that you yourself can't be all those things at once!"

**Junior,
University of Pennsylvania**

W.W.F WRESTLING — PENN STYLE

by
Sujit Suchindran
Senior, University of Pennsylvania

When I first got to school, I spent my free nights in one of two ways. I'd follow a freshman flock to a frat party, or on weekday nights, I'd scan the flyers littering the dorms for a freshman icebreaker. I first enjoyed meeting new people at these gatherings, but Trivial Pursuit tournaments gradually lost their luster and the company began to seem as stale as the food. Where had all the interesting freshmen gone, I wondered? To the *interesting* events on campus, that's where.

You have to look away from postings in elevators and restroom mirrors to find some of the greatest opportunities on campus. Don't rely on the emails the Dean sends to every freshman to find events. Scan department bulletin boards on your way to class and ask upperclassmen to forward you the emails they receive from student clubs, museums, or local music venues. If your school borders a big city, subscribe to *Time Out* magazine. Foreign language departments and student film societies screen all kinds of movies, from silent Polish art films to blockbusters. Always drop by art exhibits and author readings. If the artists disappoint you, console yourself with the free wine.

Pedantic as it sounds, I love the evening lectures Penn offers. They feature specialists in any field you're interested in and who are often famous and almost always entertaining. This was really brought home to me when I saw Alan Dershowitz debate Alan Keyes at the law school. If you're imagining two crusty academics bantering in phony British accents, think again! I'd never seen such animated—or for that matter, intelligent— speakers in my life! I felt like I was watching a W.W.F. fight break out at Socrates' School of Athens!

DON'T BE INTIMIDATED

Your school will be filled with people from all different cultures, races, and socioeconomic classes. This might be what you're used to, or it could come as somewhat of a shock. Many of the people whom you meet may have traveled the world ten times over and been exposed to opportunities and experiences you can only dream about.

> "Although I have many friends who went to prep schools, it's sometimes hard to reconcile how different our lives have been. They've traveled all around, volunteered to save the world, and had some amazing experiences. I try to keep in mind that I have those same opportunities in my future."
>
> **Sophomore,**
> **Brown University**

Don't feel intimidated by people who come from a different background than you or seem to have a broader range of experiences—look at this as an opportunity to learn and to step outside of your normal routines. Avoid the temptation to stick to people whose backgrounds are similar to yours. Some of your closest, most long-lasting friendships in college can come from people who are your complete opposite in terms of background and personality.

Remember also that other students may be on guard because they're in an unfamiliar setting and thus may come off a bit unfriendly without meaning to. Give everyone a chance to chill out and get comfortable.

MAKE YOUR OWN CHOICES

Regardless of your high school drinking practices, the availability of alcohol and the fact that you no longer have to drive home and deal with your parents after the party may change your drinking habits.

Once again, decisions about drinking—and drugs, for that matter—are ultimately your own. It's easy to be swayed by the environment and the social norms of your university. For your own sake (and for the sake of your liver), make decisions about alcohol consumption based on what's best for you, not on what everyone else is doing. If you're not comfortable with drinking or drugs, don't worry—you'll have plenty of company.

Some of your classmates who went to boarding schools may be more used to regulating themselves when it comes to drinking. In relishing your freedom and autonomy, it's easy to go crazy and wind up with consequences ranging from a bad hangover on the mild end, to a trip to the hospital, or worse, on the severe end of the spectrum. Be careful. Take your time adjusting to the party environment of your school. Make sure to take care of yourself and take care of your friends.

DARE

by
Nathaniel Bryson
Junior, Columbia University

Consider the following riddle: What shows strangers what's beneath its clothes and then shows friends what's inside its stomach? Answer: a college student who doesn't know how to drink.

At any party you can spot the freshmen whose parents sheltered them from all knowledge of sex, liquor, drugs, and other dangers in high school, only to turn them loose in college without any understanding of limits. These students go to their first party and end up in a stranger's room or, worse, a hospital bed. I don't blame these students. After all, I was one of them once.

My parents kept close tabs on me, and where they couldn't follow me, their network of informers did. In a small town like the one I grew up in, you simply don't have the freedom to break the rules and, as a consequence, you never learn to set them for yourself. I had to write a couple papers Sunday morning with earsplitting headaches in order to learn how to respect alcohol. Some people aren't so lucky. Try having to explain a $500 ambulance ride to your parents after campus police decide you need your stomach pumped. I have a friend who got kicked out of his dorm for smoking pot. He couldn't afford an apartment so he had to withdraw for a semester and this hurt his chances of getting into medical school.

As a not-so-proud DARE graduate, I know that scare tactics don't work. I think we're old enough to make our own decisions, but this isn't as simple as it sounds—it means thinking about what you're doing and seriously considering the consequences.

GET OFF CAMPUS

Whether your university happens to be in a bustling metropolis or a quaint little college town, the local community can offer an interesting and pleasant escape from the campus social scene. If there are other universities in the area, the city can be a good place to meet a wider range of people. No matter how big your campus is, or how full it is of things to do, an occasional change of scenery can provide a much-needed break from your usual routine.

Grab a few friends and go exploring. Seek out a funky little café, go dancing at a club, find an interesting theater performance, just do something different. Life on campus can sometimes begin to feel like you live in a bubble. Get some air.

WATCH YOUR EXPENSES

A college campus is probably one of the only places where you can have a great time and do a ton of different things on a tight budget.

But if your college is close to a city filled with exciting entertainment or shopping opportunities, watch out! Between hefty cover charges, overpriced food or drinks, and expensive taxis back to campus after public transportation has stopped running, a night of being out and about can get expensive—and a few too many nights or days like that can get your bank account into serious trouble.

When it comes to activities such as dinner at a nice restaurant or going to expensive clubs, you might feel a bit awkward that some of your classmates seem to have money to throw around while you're living on a tight budget. It's easy to get lured into spending more money than you should simply because that's what your friends are doing and you want to be part of the fun. We've definitely all been there.

You know your limits. Don't spend money you don't have just for the sake of not feeling left out. The majority of your fellow classmates are on tight budgets and don't have much extra cash. If your friends want to eat out, there's nothing wrong with suggesting an inexpensive restaurant. Have fun, go out, but know when you need to opt out of doing something with your friends, or suggest that you all do something less expensive.

financing your education

Financing your education can be one of the most stressful aspects of attending a top school, particularly if it's a private university. It's hard enough to get in, but once you do, the price tag to get your degree can be overwhelming for both you and your family.

Financing your education is a headache, but it's definitely doable. In addition to scholarships and financial aid from the university and outside sources, there are ways to keep yourself financially afloat throughout your undergraduate years. Below are a few general suggestions from our own experiences.

For much more specific advice about finding money to pay for school and tips on getting through college without amassing mounds of credit card debt, check out the Students Helping Students™ guide titled **GETTING THROUGH COLLEGE WITHOUT GOING BROKE**.

GET ORGANIZED
▼
CHOOSE THE RIGHT JOB
▼
AVOID WORKING TOO MUCH
▼
LOOK OUT FOR NEW SCHOLARSHIPS
▼
BE SMART WITH YOUR MONEY

GET ORGANIZED

If you're smart enough to get into your school, you're definitely smart and resourceful enough to figure out how to pay for it. By the time you read this guide, you've probably already gotten your financial aid in place and begun to save some money from your summer jobs to help pay for school. One thing to remember is that financing your college education is an ongoing process. Every year that you're at school, you'll have to make sure that your financial aid is in order, find a job, apply for new scholarships, and live on a budget.

The key is to be organized. First, make sure that you know all of the rules that apply to your financial aid:

- What forms do you and/or your parents have to fill in each year? When are they due? Where do you send them? (One example of this is the Free Application for Federal Student Aid, or the FAFSA, which you have to file every year to be eligible for financial aid, but your college or university may have other requirements.)

- Do you have to maintain a certain GPA to qualify for all or parts of your aid? What are the exact rules?

- If you've been awarded a scholarship based on your participation in a certain sport or activity, what happens to that money if you can't participate for some reason?

You should also get in the habit of regularly checking scholarship listings. Just because you're in college doesn't mean that you can't get scholarships. Every small bit helps.

Have a budget and try to stick to it. Know what you can spend and on what, and keep track of it closely. Don't deny yourself every temptation, but know when you have to pass up a night out on the town or a new CD.

Be careful with credit cards—they can easily lead you into debt, as many of us have unfortunately found out. You'll have enough loans when you graduate, and the last thing that you need is credit card debt. Don't get more than one card, choose a lower spending limit to start, and aim to pay each month's balance in full. We suggest that you seriously consider getting a debit or a check card instead of a credit card. Debit cards are linked to your checking account and that way, you can't spend more than the amount of money that you actually have.

Thinking about financial aid and budgets isn't fun, but if you get organized and know what you have to do, you'll spend less time worrying about it and run a lower risk of getting into money trouble.

CHOOSE THE RIGHT JOB

When looking for a job, start with on-campus resources, like the financial aid and the student employment offices. These places have job listings for campus organizations as well as local businesses and organizations off campus.

If you have work-study as part of your financial aid package, get to the financial aid office as soon as possible. The best jobs—those that require little effort and give you a chance to do some homework—go fast and you'll want to grab one even if you don't plan on working during the first semester.

"I really needed the money so I ran to the financial aid office, where work-study jobs were posted, as soon as I moved my stuff into my room. My roommate waited and she got stuck washing dishes in the dining hall while I landed a cushy desk job."

**Recent Grad,
Wesleyan University**

Your university may also have student agencies, which are student-run businesses and organizations that provide a variety of services ranging from laundry to film developing to bartending courses and conferences. See if any have openings that appeal to you. Also, at the beginning of each semester, keep your eyes peeled for posters advertising jobs around campus. Once you decide what kind of job you want, whether it's at the library or a research lab, go to the actual place where you'd like to work and find out if they're hiring. Some of the best jobs get filled this way and never make it to the student employment listings.

If you're not satisfied with the jobs you find on campus, or if you're looking for something different from the typical college job, check out non-campus resources.

Local newspapers always have job listings. There are also local restaurants and stores that hire students and the local magazine or newspaper might have positions available. Just keep in mind that off-campus jobs are less flexible and understanding about things like next-day exams and overdue papers.

To look for summer jobs, use your campus career center and check out online resources that can help college students find a job. Services such as monsterTRAK (**www.monstertrak.com**) and College Grad Job Hunter (**www.collegegrad.com**) are two of the most helpful.

☞ BE CREATIVE, MAKE MONEY, LEARN SOMETHING

There are many ways to make money while on campus. Consider, for example, looking for a job that's in a field that interests you and one that you want to try out for a possible career after graduation. If you're interested in the sciences or social sciences, start asking around the department to find out which faculty members need research assistants. Working in a lab can be a great way to gain expertise in the field and to get to know a faculty member.

You can also look for internships during the semester. If you're interested in writing, for example, check with the local paper—they might have a few positions available. Sometimes you'll be able to find a writing internship online and do the required work on campus. All of the writers and contributors to this guide, for example, are students who were hired by the publisher to write while still at college.

In taking on a research position or internship, it's important to understand exactly how much time you have to devote to your job. It's also important that your employer be aware of your obligations as a student and the constraints placed on your time due to academic and extracurricular commitments. You may have been able to work twenty hours a week in addition to your high school schedule, but that's not always an option in your new rigorous environment.

Another possibility for getting quick cash is picking up odd jobs. Your student employment office probably has job postings by people looking for students to help them out with a weekend move, a day of gardening, or a big party. These jobs can be a nice way to pick up extra cash without having to deal with a long-term commitment.

FRENCH LITERATURE

by
Alexandra Hardiman
Junior, Columbia University

My parents pay for my dining plan and dorm room and I cover the rest of my expenses at college. This made it hard to plan my summer following freshman year because I wanted meaningful work but couldn't afford an unpaid internship. If you're in the same bind, I have good news. As a student at a top university, you have a unique opportunity to find work that stimulates your mind and your bank account.

Employers assume that students at top schools are smart, well-trained, and hardworking, and they may offer you positions typically reserved for college graduates. I adore my French literature courses, so I fantasized about working as a translator for a French-language publisher over the summer. I applied for so many positions that I got blisters on my tongue from licking all the envelopes, but I didn't hear back from one.

It took three months of tireless job searching for a publisher to finally call. When she offered an unpaid internship for the summer, I politely yet firmly explained my financial situation. She knew an inexperienced translator could embarrass the company with even small mistakes, but she was impressed with my academic credentials and my determination, so she suggested I write sample reviews of three books and that we talk again. I slaved over the reviews and she hired me to read newly published French books and recommend those that the company should consider translating for American audiences. It seemed too good to be true—I was paid to read novels from all over the French-speaking world and share my thoughts on them! What could be more educational and entertaining?

Your own job search may be similarly long and frustrating, but remember that you don't have to wait until graduation to find meaningful employment.

AVOID WORKING TOO MUCH

Remember that your first obligation is to be a STUDENT. While financial worries can weigh heavily on your mind, it's important not to let them interfere with your college experience. Many a student has survived college on limited financial resources and you will, too. Remember that you can always work during the summer to make extra money.

While holding down a job may be a necessity, it shouldn't be something that consumes a great deal of your time. If you're finding that you keep running out of money, check your spending and see if there's anything that you can cut out.

Try not to schedule yourself to work on Friday and Saturday nights when you could be out socializing with your classmates and giving your brain a break. And if you have an exam or a big paper due and you didn't plan well, try to get someone to sub for you.

LOOK OUT FOR NEW SCHOLARSHIPS

Just because you're in college doesn't mean that you can't apply for new scholarships. Even if the amounts seem small, you already know that every small contribution helps. It will take a few hours to write an essay and fill out the application, but if you can get a few scholarships to help you and your parents pay for school, you'll have fewer loans and less debt when you graduate.

Talk to an advisor at the financial aid office and find out if your school has any resources that help you look for scholarships. There are also a number of places that you can look online, such as **www.fastweb.com**.

> "*Financing a private school education can be difficult, and even stressful. So, scholarships are key! Applying usually doesn't take more than an hour or so, and the fiscal rewards can be amazing! Although $1,000 may not seem to put a dent in that $38,000 bill, every bit helps. The money you earn will add up very quickly!*"

> **Sophomore,**
> **Dartmouth College**

BE SMART WITH YOUR MONEY

Most college students live on a budget, although it might not seem so if you see your roommate spending money on everything from new socks to a new convertible and then calling up daddy to ask for a couple extra grand for that fabulous spring break trip to the Bahamas. To make it through school without amassing huge amounts of credit card debt, you have to watch what you spend.

We suggest that you put together a really simple budget that's easy to follow. Figure out what expenses you absolutely have to pay each semester—tuition, room and board, textbooks, clothes, etc.—and where you'll get the money to pay for them—parents, your savings, financial aid, job. Be realistic when calculating these and leave yourself some wiggle room for those few unexpected purchases, such as a replacement for your dead Discman or the hefty charge for losing a library book. If you have more resources than expenses, you're in luck—you can either save this money or spend it on fun things like shopping or going out.

Be creative about saving money at school. Buy used books and sell your own at the end of each semester if you don't think you'll use them again. Go shopping in thrift stores and sell them your old clothes. Saving money doesn't have to be a chore, and you really can make it fun if you try.

MONTHLY BUDGET TEMPLATE

Here's a quick template that you can use to create your monthly budget. In most cases, you'll pay tuition and room and board once every semester, so we won't include these expenses in the monthly budget. You should know how much money you have to save during the year and each month to pay for your share of tuition and room and board, so we've included that as an expense —you should think of it that way and try to put that amount of money in the bank each month.

Expenses		Resources	
Savings Contribution		Work-Study	
Books/School Supplies		Savings Account	
Meals (if not already paid in meal plan)		Other	
Take-out/Going out			
Car Expenses			
Other Travel Expenses			
Phone/Internet			
Clothes			
Other			

WRITE IT DOWN! You might think that you can remember where you spent your money, but things tend to slip your memory and having a record is extremely helpful to see when you're reaching your limit. As you keep track of your monthly expenses, it might help to stick to the same categories you created in your budget— so a meal out would go into the Take-out/Going Out category.

FUN: WORK-STUDY STYLE

by
Elisa Leslie Barquin
Senior, Columbia University

I went to Columbia expecting to step out of class and into a *Sex and the City* episode. So did many of my new friends from private schools, but they had one thing I didn't: daddy's credit card. I couldn't follow my new friends to glitzy clubs and Fifth Avenue shopping sprees on my work-study budget. I felt so uncultured. After all, I'd never seen Sarah Jessica Parker stay in and rent a movie because she was strapped for cash.

While money sometimes limits your options, you still don't need a lot of it to have a good time. Set a budget for each week so that you don't run out of money halfway through the semester and feel *completely* deprived. Save money over the summer if at all possible so you can splurge now and then. Learn how to cut corners. I saved money by using the library's course reserves and studied there to avoid the distractions of my dorm room. Saving a buck here and there really adds up. This seems obvious, but it took me way too long to buy a mug and tea bags instead of picking up a drink en route to class. Every two weeks, my Starbucks addiction was costing as much as an exciting night out, and hot water out of my own microwave tastes almost as good.

But above all, remember that it's okay to tell friends that you're not up for a high-rolling night. If someone can't understand that other people must operate on a budget, do you really want to spend time with them anyway? Plan an activity you can afford and then invite your friends along. That way you don't even need to mention money. My friends and I used to go out for beers and burgers after Friday class, but by the end of first semester I could no longer afford to join them. Instead of guilt-tripping them to the cafeteria, I suggested we grill in a nearby park. We enjoyed better tasting meat, fresh air, and a new experience. Now picnics in the park are a Friday afternoon tradition.

the daily grind

Making the transition from public high school to a top-notch university can be difficult, tumultuous, but ultimately very rewarding. Here are a few ideas to help you stay sane during your initial months on campus.

▶TAKE IT EASY

If you've come from a laidback community with a laidback high school, the fast-paced environment of your university can be a bit of a shock. It's easy to get caught up in the pressurized atmosphere and find yourself stressing about anything and everything from academics and social life to the food and your wardrobe.

Take a deep breath and relax. Whether or not you have the time to finish the reading for next day's lecture isn't going to make or break your grade in the class. Not having the perfect outfit to wear to an event doesn't mean that you're committing social suicide. Sometimes, it's easy to let yourself take things too seriously. Set your own pace and your own goals and stick to them.

▶DON'T BE TOO HARD ON YOURSELF

College is hard for EVERYONE—at least at first. One of the toughest parts of surviving at a top university is that everyone *pretends* to be totally put together and on top of everything. We'll let you in on a little secret: They're not. If you feel like you're the only one who's having difficulty then you're wrong. Almost everyone else is also struggling—they've just gotten good at not showing it.

The adjustment is tough and the first semester of your freshman year will be a difficult one. Don't beat yourself up if you're still feeling homesick in November and December. It will take a while to create a supportive network of friends and faculty similar to what you had at home, but once you do, life will settle down and things will go much more smoothly.

▶BALANCE

Balance is probably the single most important skill that you can learn in order to survive at college and beyond. The days of being able to do it all and be the best at everything are gone. Most of your classes will give you more work than you can possibly finish and, if you spend all of your time trying to read every word of every assignment and drafting every paper to perfection, you'll be missing out on other great parts of your college experience.

You shouldn't feel guilty about fudging a reading assignment in order to go celebrate a friend's birthday once in a while. Once you get a feel for your academic style and figure out what you need to do in order to do well academically, give yourself a break and spend some time focusing on social and extracurricular pursuits. You have the privilege of attending one of the top universities in the country where you're surrounded by some of the most amazing young people in the world. Make sure to spend time with them!

▶FIGURE OUT WHAT YOU WANT

What your college experience will be like depends in a very significant way on what you make of it. While it's easy to become overwhelmed with everything you have to do, take some time to think about what you'd like to get out of your time at school, your classes, your extracurriculars, your entire experience, and out of the near future in your life. Think about it, but most importantly, go after it.

Guilt is a very powerful feeling, and if you spend your time feeling guilty about not taking the classes your parents want you to take or leaving an activity that you've been with since freshman year, you're denying yourself the whole purpose of the college experience: the education of you.

The four years fly by. Many students take time off during their college years in order to gain perspective and recharge their minds and their souls. If you need to slow down, change classes or activities, or take time off, by all means, do so. For the first time, you're pretty much completely in charge of your life and your choices.

▶ DON'T BE SCARED

Your university will be filled with new experiences and new situations, new people, and new ideas. It's very comforting to stick with what you've always known. While it's important to have a home base where you're comfortable, you also never know what or who may be out there. Don't deny yourself amazing experiences simply because you're afraid. The more risks you take and the more new ground you explore, the more you'll learn—about others and yourself.

what "they" say

Many people recognize that the transition from public high school to a selective university can be challenging and intimidating. Here are a few words of wisdom and encouragement from deans, admissions officers, and professors at Harvard University, Princeton University, Stanford University, and Yale University.

WHAT IS THE ONE PIECE OF ADVICE YOU WOULD GIVE TO STUDENTS MAKING THE TRANSITION FROM PUBLIC HIGH SCHOOL TO A TOP UNIVERSITY?

"Be confident in your abilities. It's impossibly tough to get in, and if you got in, then you're good enough to succeed at the school."

"Trust your public high school training. You're at no disadvantage."

"The faculty teaching you, even at the best universities, themselves come from very diverse backgrounds and will be prepared to evaluate you on the work and effort you put out. They will want to help you succeed—positive achievement makes a faculty member feel good, and makes their job easier."

"Good time management skills are essential. And part of that is learning to adapt—or, in some cases, upgrade—the study habits you employed in your best moments in high school, to meet the new challenges of university course work, and the distractions of university extracurricular life."

"Most private universities are very selective, and they have rigid admission criteria—thus you have 'passed' rigorous screening and are as capable as anyone coming from a private school. Don't feel inferior—because you are not."

"It's very much like the difference between playing college sports and playing professional sports. You were the best of the best on your college team. You get to the NBA or NFL and guess what? Everybody was the best of the best. It's a whole new ballgame. The one equalizer for all students, regardless of high school prep, is TIME. There are those who manage it well and those who don't quite get the handle. In adjusting to an elite university, any student who doesn't learn how to pick up the pace and manage time without the structure of a daily high school routine is in trouble."

WHAT IS THE TOUGHEST OBSTACLE STUDENTS FACE WHEN GOING FROM A PUBLIC HIGH SCHOOL TO A TOP U.?

"Learning not to be intimidated by the reputation or the hype surrounding the preparation some fellow students may have gotten from attending prep schools, or by coming from relatively more privileged backgrounds."

"Thinking/feeling that they're less prepared than others who've "prepped." Thirty years ago Harvard did a study of performance of public school "admits" compared to prep school admits. Finding: Prep school students had an edge in performance...for ONE semester (due to more concentrated prep school work on writing college-type papers, and due to a bit more experience in learning how to "work the system"). But after one semester it's a totally level playing field!"

"Usually, private high schools have smaller classes and the students have been asked to write more and take more essay exams. If the bulk of your exams have been of the multiple choice variety, taking a three-hour essay exam is quite a challenge and requires a much different kind of studying."

HOW CAN STUDENTS BEST PREPARE THEMSELVES TO MAKE THE TRANSITION FROM PUBLIC HIGH SCHOOL TO A TOP UNIVERSITY?

"Think about the goals and priorities you have, and the motivations that stand behind them: What do you want to get out of the university experience? But also be prepared to be realistic and adapt or reassess them, after you've been a school for a year or two. Being conscious of the resources and motivations you bring from your family and personal background is always relevant—they'll always be with you."

"Work on entering with confidence, trusting your public high school training."

"Take the most rigorous courses offered in your high school—opt for the writing intensive classes—really work on your writing skills, and if you read slowly, work on building up your speed as well as retention. Also get used to asking for help if you need it. Utilize office hours, tutoring, and group study—whatever resources the university offers. It's a sign of strength, not weakness, to do so."

"Come in with a mindset that helps you to know that you deserve to be at an elite school. Seek out places of support as soon as you arrive on campus—places like an advising center, tutoring center, ethnic center, career counseling center. Jump into as many study groups as you can and, most importantly, get to know the faculty who teach you, whether the classes are large or small. Having a faculty friend/mentor could be the difference between a great college experience and an okay one."

helpful resources

Here are a few other resources you might want to consider as you make the transition from a public high school to your top university.

 BOOKS

Making the Most of College: Students Speak Their Minds, by Richard J. Light. Harvard University Press, 2001.

An award-winning book written by a Harvard professor who interviewed 1600 students over the course of 10 years, *Making the Most of College* provides insight on a variety of topics, ranging from study skills to classes to college life in general. Filled with anecdotes from students themselves, Light's book has enjoyed much success and makes for an interesting and enlightening read.

Major in Success: Make College Easier, Fire up Your Dreams, and Get a Very Cool Job, by Patrick Combs. Ten Speed Press, 2000.

A smart, inspirational, and energetic guide to figuring out what makes you tick and how to turn it into something you can do with your life. Written by a recent grad, this book is a great resource.

What Smart Students Know: Maximum Grades, Optimum Learning, Minimum Time, by Adam Robinson. Crown Publishing, 1993.

You're smart enough to get into your top U., but you can still learn a thing or two from this book. Its main argument is that succeeding at academics isn't something that certain students are gifted with, but something that many students can learn how to do.

☞ WEBSITES

www.princetonreview.com/college

This service from the Princeton Review ranks the 345 best colleges. It's fun to type in the name of your chosen school to see where it ranks. It's also a good way to find out the strengths and weaknesses of your school before you get there.

www.edu.com

This is the Student Advantage Tech Store, and it's a good website to buy computers and other electronic equipment at discount prices for students.

www.fastweb.com

On this site you can search for scholarships and get tips on financial aid and careers. And all of its extensive services are free.

the final word

"The four years of college are an incredible time to build yourself and figure out who it is you think you are or want to be. It's sometimes harder to figure that out when you have people around you reminding you of who they knew you were, or who YOU knew you were in high school. Coming from a public school you're less likely to bring company to your university, and that just might be best."

**Junior,
Harvard University**

Some people will tell you that the hardest part about a selective university is getting in. That may be true, but making the transition from high school to that university is also a challenging experience. It's one of those experiences where you'll look back and realize how much you grew during that time.

Don't waste your time worrying or feeling sorry about the fact that you may not have the academic background of some of your private school classmates. You'll catch up quickly and, in the long run, your overall performance in college has less to do with your high school background and more with what you make of your college experience.

It's important to face the transition, and college in general, with your head up, eyes open, shoulders back, and feet firmly planted on the ground—ready to take on anything and everything that comes your way. And above all, remember to keep your sense of humor!

To learn more about **Students Helping Students™**
guides, read samples and student-written articles, share
your own experiences with other students, suggest a topic
or ask questions, visit us at
www.StudentsHelpingStudents.com!

We're always looking for fresh minds and new ideas!